# Sunshine
## & SUBCLASSES

AUSTRALIAN IMMIGRATION EXPLAINED

by Mege Dalton

ISBN: 1491018615

ISBN-13: 978-1491018613

## Dedication

For Miila.

# *Contents*

# Acknowledgments

There are so many people that contributed to the writing of this book. To all the clients I have helped over the years, thank you for entrusting me with your future hopes and dreams. It has been a privilege to work with you all and I have learned so much in the process.

To Greg Sheppard my first legal mentor in Port Moresby from whom I learned so much, and George Fox in Brisbane who walked me through the maze that is the business visa process at the beginning and helped me get under my own steam; thank you both so much.

To my team here at The Immigration Agency who helped with the technical proof read for this book, ensuring every T was crossed and every i was dotted when it came to the visa regulations, and criteria; thank you, Colin Maguire, Yana Panchuk and Grainne Coyne.

Thanks also to Betty for her seasoned editorial input. And finally thanks to my husband John without whose unwavering support this book would never have happened.

# Section 1    The Big Picture

MEGE DALTON

# Introduction

Hello and welcome to the beginning of your journey to Australian permanent residency. If you dream of living and working in Australia but you don't know where to start, or how to go about it, take heart because you are not alone, my name is Mege Dalton and I was once in your shoes. Not literally of course because that would be, well, weird.

I was once in your shoes figuratively because, like you, I wasn't born in Australia. I was born in Papua New Guinea, a large island just north of Australia. PNG, as most Australians refer to it, was once a colony of Australia and there is a long tradition of ties between the two countries.

My mother is a Doctor and when I was growing up she spent time working in some of the major hospitals in Sydney. My sisters and I accompanied her on these contracts. When it was time for me to go to high school I went to New England Girls' School, which is located in northern New South Wales.

In many ways you could say I grew up in Australia, yet I didn't become an Australian Citizen until 2006 and this gives me a unique perspective. I know Australia from the inside and from the outside. I know what it's like to want to live and work there permanently, and what it's like to go through the migration process. This perspective is crucial in my work as an Australian lawyer specializing in migration law.

In my time as a registered migration agent I have helped hundreds of people navigate the migration process and achieve their dream of living and working in Australia. I've worked in Australia as a migration agent, or *on shore*, as it is called, and I've worked *off shore* too in Ireland, where my husband, John, is from. It was in Ireland that I started my migration company, The Immigration Agency.

Over the years I've talked to literally thousands of people about their visa options. What I come across, again and again, is a basic lack of understanding of how the Australian visa system works in practice and how it applies to the specific individual. There is no shortage of information about the Australian visa system, the Internet is awash with it, but information is not understanding.

As Forrest Gump's mother used to say, "Life is like a box of chocolates." His aunt, on the other hand, used to say, "Life is like a box of Lego, and on that box is a picture of a beautiful model of the Taj Mahal made out of 1,000 Lego blocks. Inside the box are the 1,000 Lego blocks that go to make up the model. Now Forrest, if you have no instruction booklet to show you how to put the blocks together you will never make the Taj Mahal." You can see why she didn't make it into the movie but her point is valid.

The Taj Mahal for many people is the dream of living

and working in Australia. The Lego blocks are the individual pieces of information about the visa application process all, as I said, freely available.

My intention for this book is to provide you with the instruction booklet. I will show you how the blocks go together and help you understand the visa process. This book combines all the information about the Australian migration process with my experience of how the system works in practice and distills it down to an understandable form.

From experience I know you will be only really interested in the parts of this book that relate to you and that's fine; feel free to hop around, in fact I encourage it.

I have divided the book into four sections.

Section One covers the overarching principals at work within and behind the migration process. It also includes a quick run through the more popular visas and introduces the concept of strategy in your visa application.

Section Two covers what I call the nuts and bolts. These are the separate components that are required for inclusion with most visa applications. This section includes chapters about police clearances, medical checks, English language ability, State sponsorship, and how the SkillSelect system works.

Section Three covers the main visa subclasses. If you're not sure which visa you might be eligible for you can get an overview in Chapter 3 - Which Visa?

Section Four covers the further considerations of citizenship, finding a migration agent and what to do if you overstay your visa.

I wish you every success in achieving your dream of living and working in Australia.

Mege Dalton

# 1 The Big Decision Myth

Frank slumped in his chair. "You're kidding me."

"I wish I was Frank, but I'm not."

"You're telling me I can't get a visa?"

"Not a skilled independent visa, no."

"But I'm in demand --- I mean carpenters are in demand."

"Yes, carpenters are on the occupations in demand list. . ."

"And I have plenty of experience. Over ten years."

"Yes, your experience is fine."

"And I still can't get a visa?"

"No, not a skilled independent visa, but you may have other visa options."

"This is unbelievable."

Frank was a victim of what I call The Big Decision Myth. He had thought long and hard about emigration. He had talked about it with his wife Betty at length. They had considered the implications it would have on their respective parents, who were getting on in years, and what it would mean to their friends and family. They particularly agonised about the effects it would have on their children, especially their teenage daughter Mary, who was at an age where her friends were her life.

Frank had seen his former workmates emigrate. The young ones were the first to leave but over time the older, more experienced men had gone too. These were Frank's contemporaries; men he had gone to technical school with. Frank and Betty kept waiting for things to improve but after 14 months of unemployment their situation had become desperate and they couldn't afford to stay. Any patriotic feelings Frank once had about sticking it out through the bad times were now a luxury.

He knew there was plenty of work for carpenters in Australia and eventually, he and Betty made the hard decision to emigrate. That's when they got in touch with me.

After all that thought and consideration the last thing Frank expected to hear was that getting a visa was going to be an issue. He was also shocked at how much the whole process was going to cost and how long it would take. He had the impression his friends had just picked up the phone to Australia and said, "Alright I'm coming."

As I have observed it The Big Decision Myth arises out of two things; an assumption and a fear. The assumption has to do with choice. Frank and Betty had spent the whole time making their decision based on the assumption that getting a visa would be easy. They assumed they had a choice. The fear comes from the erroneous idea that if you are approved for a visa you will have to leave for Australia immediately or risk losing your visa.

This is not the case at all. For most permanent visas there will be a specific date by which you have to activate your visa and usually that date coincides with the 12 month anniversary of when you completed your medicals and police checks. To activate your visa you simply have to enter Australia.

Let's say you completed your medicals and police checks in March and your 4 year skilled independent visa is approved in June, you have until March of the following year to enter Australia and activate your visa. The clock on your 4 years wouldn't start until then.

Once you have entered Australia and activated your visa it is up to you when to make the permanent move to Australia. It could be at the time you enter or it could be months later.

Sadly I have seen so many people wait until all other avenues have been exhausted, holding off for as long as they could before finally making the big decision to emigrate only to discover they have left it too late. They no longer meet one or more of the requirements needed to apply for a visa. So when they were spending all that time arriving at the decision to migrate, the choice they assumed they had was in fact slipping through their fingers.

If Frank and Betty had begun the application process as soon as they began to consider moving to Australia, then by the time they were ready to make a decision they would have had a real choice.

Don't make the same mistake. Rather than beginning the application process once you have decided, obtain good advice while you are deciding, so you can make a decision based on real options.

Remember, just because you are approved for an Australian visa doesn't mean you have to go, but you definitely won't be able to go if you don't have a visa so . . start now.

## 2 The System

Mary slammed her hands on the desk, "God almighty, do they not want people to go to Australia at all?"

"They do of course Mary, they just want people with certain skills. . ."

". . . and experience and age and education. Is there a fashion sense criteria?"

"No Mary, there isn't."

I'd spent the last twenty minutes explaining to Mary why her visa options were considerably fewer than she had thought. It was her first encounter with the Australian migration system and I could understand her frustration. Mary was verbalising a sentiment I see many of my clients quietly harbor, the feeling that the system is purposefully complex, difficult, convoluted, and downright nit picky.

Her conclusion was incorrect of course; Australia wants people now more than ever.

To understand why the system is the way it is you need to understand the history that shaped it and the political pressure that particular history brings to bear on it to this day.

Immigration policy in Australia has been a political hot potato going back as far as the federation of Australia in 1901. The infamous White Australia Policy was instituted at the time to try and stop the influx of Chinese migrants flocking to the country during the Australian gold rush of the mid 1900's. Though the expression, "White Australia Policy," was never officially used, the series of policies that went to comprise it effectively excluded all non-Europeans from immigrating into Australia. The White Australia Policy was actively in effect from the 1890's through to the 1950's.

It wasn't until the 1970's that things began to change. The last vestiges of the White Australia Policy were swept away as Australia reconciled itself to the reality that the country was comprised of more than just white Anglo Saxons of the Crocodile Dundee variety. It began to redefine itself as a country that was comprised of many ethnic groups and it was this mix of races that gave the country its rich cultural texture. A new multicultural immigration policy was formulated enshrining this new identity.

Australia could afford to become more egalitarian in its migration policy because it had a new threat landing on its beaches every week - refugees. Successive Governments could take the focus off the legal migration figures easily because every week there was a new lurid story about people risking life and limb, setting out in flimsy boats across open water, to try and land in Australia illegally. This was much more emotive, sound-bite-worthy stuff. It even won an election for former Prime Minister, John Howard, when he did a textbook piece of misdirection just before the 2001 election by drawing media attention to a case where boat people bound for Australia had purportedly thrown their children overboard when approached by the coast guard. It was such an incendiary story it gave John Howard a free pass to a landslide victory at the polls. It's still a touchy subject with Australians and not one to bring up in a pub unless you want a fight.

Ross Gittins, an economist at the time commented that, "Minister John Howard had been a tricky chap on immigration by appearing tough on illegal immigration to win support from the working class, while simultaneously winning support from employers with high legal immigration."

And that is the nub of the issue to this day; Immigration is, and always has been, a balancing act for the Australian Government. On the one hand they need to appease voter concerns about Australian workers losing out to immigrants, while on the other hand they need to allow the Australian employers to get the workers they need.

Migration policy writhes back and forth changing every six months or so trying to make as many of the people happy for as much of the time as possible, or at least until the next election.

It makes for an overly reactive system because in my observation the majority of changes to the migration system have political origins.

Here is one small example to give you an idea of how it works. At the moment China is a major trading partner with Australia. The current mining boom in Australia is largely fuelled by China's demand for raw materials. Australia's economy is thriving so no worries mate.

What is not so obvious is that the mining boom is only happening in very specific regions of Australia and by and large these are away from the major cities. Most of the voting public live in the major cities and their perception is different. What they are seeing is Chinese millionaires purchasing large blocks of downtown real estate.

For example, Australian real estate agents CBRE estimate that Chinese buyers account for 85% of recent large sales of sites in and around the Melbourne CBD to the value of more than $4 billion AUD.

The same media that whipped up the electorate about the boat people is now in a frenzy that Australia is being bought up by China. This kind of hysteria harks back to the roots of the white Australia policy and is something the Government has to consider carefully when formulating its migration policy.

With multiculturalism now a sacred tenet of Australian political identity the Government have to be very careful not to look as if it is excluding any nationality for no good reason. They have to find ways to appease both sides without appearing partial to either.

Their solutions are usually subtle.

For example, what I have observed in the last five years is an increase in the English language test requirements and a bias of the points test in favor of excellent English speakers.

The result of this will be that when your average Australian voter walks into a shop and is served by someone other than a fair dinkum Aussie battler (white anglo saxon), at least the person they are dealing with will be able to speak to them in a reasonably high standard of English.

The knock on effect of these changes off shore, half a world away, is that in countries where English is the first language like the UK or Ireland, for example, the English language requirements have become so onerous that some of the native English speakers in these countries often have to sit the English test two or three times before they get the required score. From their perspective this is utterly crazy, and without an understanding of the origins of the requirement I can see why they would think so.

As I said the visa system can change every six months or so, and any aspect of the system can change, from what skills are in demand, to the cost of applications. Australia has a Federal Government, which has jurisdiction over the whole country, and then each State or Territory has its own Government also. Changes can take place at State and Federal level. It all depends on which way the political balancing act is going.

The main issue the current Government is grappling with is meeting the massive demand for skilled workers by the mining industry without inadvertently opening the floodgates into the rest of the country.

The skilled visa system was completely overhauled in July 2012 in an attempt to address this issue and so far it seems to be working. I have never seen skilled workers processed so quickly. In one case I had a client go from initial application to working in Australia in under a month!

Once you understand that the visa system is going to change regularly, and you understand why it changes, you can begin to get a feel for what changes may be coming based on the political climate in Australia. At the very least it will give you some understanding of why the system is the way it is.

# 3 What visa?

The easiest way to get a visa to Australia is to meet the requirements for that visa. I know that's a bit like saying the easiest way to win the lottery is to have the right numbers but it's true, the easiest visas to get have the fewest requirements.

To help you understand where you fit in the visa system let me quickly run through the most common Australian visas starting with the easiest one to get first and work through to the hardest.

### Tourist visa

Depending on your nationality all you need for this visa is an airline ticket. If you are a citizen of one of the countries or regions listed below, you can apply for this visa, or ETA (Electronic Travel Authority) as it is called, through a travel agent, airline, specialist service provider or an Australian visa office outside Australia.

Andorra
Austria
Belgium

Brunei
Canada
Denmark
Finland
France
Germany
Greece
Hong Kong (SAR)
Iceland
Ireland
Italy
Japan
Liechtenstein
Luxembourg
Malaysia
Malta
Monaco
The Netherlands
Norway
Portugal
Republic of San Marino
Singapore
South Korea
Spain
Sweden
Switzerland
Taiwan
United Kingdom - British Citizen
United Kingdom - British National (Overseas)
United States of America
Vatican City

This visa is valid for 3 months. You can get an extension of up to 12 months, in 3 month increments, but for each successive 3 month block you may need to demonstrate sufficient funds to cover your stay. There are no work rights with this visa.

### Working holiday visa

All you need for this visa is to be between 18 and 30 years of age, be a citizen of one of the approved countries and have $5,000 AUD in your bank account. There is a list of the approved countries in Chapter 14 – Working Holiday Visa.

### Spouse visa

All you need for this visa is an Australian spouse.

### Family sponsorship visa

All you need for this visa is an Australian family member willing to sponsor you.

### Employer sponsored visa

All you need for this visa is an Australian employer who wants you, specifically, to come and work for them.

### Business visa

There are a couple of variations but in essence all you need for this visa is to have assets worth between $800,000 and $2,250,000 Australian dollars, have a business with an annual turnover of at least $500,000 Australian dollars and have a successful business background.

### General Skilled Visa

I'm a glass-half-full kind of woman so I'm not saying it's the hardest visa to get but it's certainly not the easiest.

All you need for this is visa is to have a skill that is in demand, current experience in that skill, a high level of English and possibly a State that wants to sponsor you.

I will go into each visa in more detail in the following chapters. If you are put off by the requirements for the visa you were interested in, bear this in mind, Australia allocated 185,000 visas in 2012 and all were filled. Which means 185,000 people met the various requirements.

Without wishing to sound like an ad for the lottery, this year it could be you.

# 4 Strategy

Bill looked left and right conspiratorially, "Really? Will that work?"

"Definitely," I replied.

Bill had come to see me with low expectations. He had done his research and as far as he could make out he was ineligible for a visa. He had a good job, experience and a qualification in electronics. The problem was his occupation wasn't on the list of occupations in demand for Australia.

I had reviewed Bill's qualifications and experience comprehensively. I realised that his qualifications combined with his experience as a manager would result in a positive assessment, not as an electronics engineer, but as a business machine mechanic. This was an occupation that was on the list of occupations in demand for Australia.

The plan I had just laid out for Bill was to get him positively assessed as a business machine mechanic with

State sponsorship, and to then apply for a State sponsored skilled migration visa.

I'm happy to say Bill went for the plan and he is now living and working in Australia.

Bill's story highlights an aspect of visa application that is often overlooked - strategy. It is understandable that you could, in the face of the overwhelming amount of information and criteria, follow your application possibilities to their logical conclusion, just like Bill had, and decide that you were ineligible. Sometimes it is not the case. With a bit of creative strategy and connecting seemingly unrelated dots, a lot is possible. Granted you may need the help of a registered migration agent to show you how to connect the dots but there are often possibilities that may not be obvious.

Strategy applies to the whole process of migrating to Australia. It is important to have a plan for your application including all the logistical details you will need to take care of at the 3, 6, 9 and 12 month milestones before your departure.

Before you even start your application there are some basic things you need to check. These may sound obvious but you'd be surprised at the number of people who don't check them.

For example, if you have any serious medical conditions check that they are not going to interfere with your migration plans. If you have any prior criminal convictions you will need to get the official record so you have clear details, get the court transcript or apply for your police clearance to see what is listed on it. You'd be amazed how many people with charges don't know the clear details or what the charges are.

Other logistics include making sure you have at least 2 years left on your passport before you begin your application.

It is important to find all your paperwork and get certified copies of everything. The Immigration Department won't accept any original documents. Include birth and marriage certificates, employment references, passport(s) and qualifications.

If you are going to apply for a spouse visa start collecting evidence of your relationship now, this includes joint bank statements, joint lease agreements, photos of the two of you together, anything that will help the case officer reviewing your case to see you have a genuine relationship. This is required for both de facto or married relationship applicants.

If you are on a working holiday visa, plan to do the 3-month farm work section early, if you leave it to the last 3 months you will run out of time and seriously limit your possibilities for finding a suitable employer, which in turn will limit your chances for renewing your visa for a second year.

Strategy is an important aspect of the application process and I will make reference to it throughout the book as it relates to the visa subclass in each chapter, but before we get into that we need to go through the various requirements common to most visa categories.

# Section 2    Nuts and Bolts

# 5 Points Testing

Living in Europe has kind of ruined me when it comes to the Australian points test system. I blame the Eurovision Song contest. Every year it explodes into our living room in a blaze of techno kitsch and pyrotechnics. It all builds towards the results tally at the end of the contest with voting from the participating juries around Europe. Through a shaky satellite link up a national celebrity will deliver the scores from their juries in accents of varying degrees of clarity, but it doesn't matter because the studio host will repeat the scores and then repeat them again in French for good measure.

"Norway eight points," says the regional judge.
"Norvège huit points," the studio host repeats, to wild applause from the crowd, especially the Norwegians.
"Germany ten points."
"Allemagne dix points."
"Ireland twelve points."
"Irlande douse points." Unbridled joy erupts in Ireland.

It is such a high intensity event that it has imprinted itself on my subconscious and surfaces whenever I'm calculating points for clients. I find myself thinking like the Eurovision results tally.

40 years old, fifteen points.
Quarante ans, quinze points.
Bachelors Degree, fifteen points.
Diplôme d'enseignement supérieur, quinze points.

I've had to stop myself saying the points in French to clients a few times.

On reflection I think my mind is trying to make a pretty boring aspect of the visa process more interesting. Thankfully not all visas are points tested, but for the ones that are, the points test is the main criteria for eligibility. Beyond eligibility, your points score can be the deciding factor in how long it takes for your expression of interest (EOI) to get accepted, but more on that later. Currently the minimum points required for most points tested visas is between 60 and 65 points.

So without further ado here are the votes from the participating criteria. Sorry, can't help myself.

### Age
Always a popular criteria and unlike all the others it is the only one you can't do anything about.

Between 18 and 24 years?  - 25 points.
Between 25 and 32 years?  - 30 points.
Between 33 and 39 years?  - 25 points.
Between 40 and 44 years?  - 15 points.
Between 45 and 49 years?  -  0 points.

As you can see you get the most points if you are between 25 and 32.

**English language ability**

If you are from an English speaking country you might think there is no need for you to do an English language test but when you consider the points awarded for the test scores you begin to see how you can use the test strategically to add points to your overall points test score.

The standard test for English language ability is called IELTS (International English Language Testing System). There is another test called OET (Occupational English Test) but this is only available to health care practitioners.

In the IELTS test there are three levels of score - competent, proficient and superior, and the points are allocated as follows -

Competent - 0 points

(While a competent IELTS score will receive no points, applicants from non-English speaking countries are required to provide a competent score before their visa is awarded. A competent score is also a minimum requirement for sponsorship by some Australian States.)

Proficient  - 10 points

Superior    - 20 points

The test is divided into 4 components, reading, writing, speaking and listening. Each component is scored individually and the scores from the 4 components are combined to give an average score.

To get a **Competent** score you need to get a score of at least 6 in each of the four components.

To get a **Proficient** score you need to get a score of at least 7 in each of the four components.

To get a **Superior** score you need to get a score of at least 8 in each of the four components.

Make no mistake, the IELTS is not easy. I've had a number of clients who are native speakers who have had to retake the IELTS test twice and three times until they got the score they needed. The main thing to remember about the IELTS test is how you can use it to boost your overall points score.

### Skilled Employment
You get a certain amount of points if you have employment experience in an occupation that is in demand. Which occupations are in demand changes regularly and varies from State to State. You are awarded points based on verifiable evidence of your skilled employment history. Your employment experience can be either in Australia or another country and you will score different points depending on which.

For skilled employment within Australia
| | |
|---|---|
| 1 year in the past 10 | - 5 points |
| 3 years in the past 10 | - 10 points |
| 5 years in the past 10 | - 15 points |
| 8 years in the past 10 | - 20 points |

For skilled employment outside of Australia
| | |
|---|---|
| 3 years in the past 10 | - 5 points |
| 5 years in the past 10 | - 10 points |
| 8 years in the past 10 | - 15 points |

You can combine skilled employment within Australia and skilled employment overseas, however the maximum number of points you can score for this criteria is still 20 points.

### Educational Qualifications
You are awarded points for the highest qualification you have attained. For example, if you have obtained both a Bachelors Degree and a Doctorate Degree, you can only

claim points for the Doctorate Degree.

## Qualification Points

| | |
|---|---|
| PhD; Overseas PhD | - 20 points |
| Bachelors Degree, or Bachelor + Masters/Honours | - 15 points |
| Diploma, AQF III/IV or trade qualification | - 10 points |

Qualifications earned overseas need to be recognised as comparable to the relevant Australian level qualifications. This will usually happen during the skills assessment phase for your nominated occupation.

It's worth noting that you may also be able to claim points for a qualification unrelated to your nominated occupation.

### Sponsored Category

If you apply under the Skilled Sponsored category you may receive extra points for being sponsored by an Australian State or Territory Government.

## State/Territory Sponsorship Points

If you are nominated by a State or Territory Government under a State Migration Plan, subclass 190, you receive
- 5 points

If you are nominated by a State or Territory Government under a State Migration Plan, or an eligible relative, to a designated area (subclass 487 or 475 Skilled-Regional Sponsored visas) you receive        - 10 points

An eligible family member may sponsor you under a subclass 190 or subclass 886 visa, but no points are awarded.

In the next section we get into the more obscure points

allocations. They don't apply to most people but I include them here in case they apply to you.

### Australian Qualifications

You are awarded points if you have completed an Australian qualification from an Australian educational institution. You must have earned this qualification while you were in Australia. The course of study must have been full time, and at least two years in length.

### Australian Qualifications Points

Met the two year study requirement while in Australia
- 5 points

### Regional Study

If you meet the two-year Australian study requirement listed above while you were living and studying in a designated "Regional" area of Australia you receive a further                                  - 5 points

### Completion of a Professional Year

A professional year is a structured professional development program, which combines formal training with on-the-job experience. If you have completed an approved professional year in your nominated occupation you receive                                  - 5 points

### Language Skills

If you have NAATI-approved translator/interpreter-level language skills in one of Australia's designated community languages you receive                                  - 5 points

### Spouse Skills

If your spouse also satisfies the basic visa requirements and has obtained a suitable skills assessment from the relevant assessing authority you receive a further
- 5 points

How it all fits together.

Let me give you a few examples to show you how points are calculated and how you can be strategic about getting the most points possible.

### Bill

Bill is a 32 year old Irish carpenter with 8 years experience who wants to live in Perth.

Here is how Bills points score would be calculated. Because he is aged between 25 and 32 years he gets
- 30 points.

Because he has 8 years experience outside Australia in the past 10 years in an occupation that is in demand he gets
- 15 points,
so now his total points score is          - 45 points.

Because he has attained a trade qualification outside Australia he gets a further          - 10 points,
so now his total points score is          - 55 points.

Because he is nominated for State sponsorship by Western Australia he gets a further          - 5 points,
so now his total points score is          - 60 points.

Let's look at another case.

### Jinu

Jinu is a 41 year old Indian Nurse with 15 years experience. She obtained her nursing degree in Australia and has worked in various countries since. She currently lives in the UK and wants to migrate to Sydney.

Here is how Jinu points score would be calculated.

Because she is aged between 40 and 44 years old she gets
- 15 points.

Because she has 8 years experience outside Australia in the past 10 years in an occupation that is in demand she gets 15 points, plus she has 1 years experience working in Australia in the last 5 years so she gets another 5 points for this which brings her total work experience points to
- 20 points.
Her total points score now is                          - 35 points.

Because she has obtained a Bachelor Degree she gets 15 points and because that degree was obtained in Australia and the course was longer than 2 years she gets a further 5 points which brings her overall qualifications score to
- 20 points.
Her total points score is now                          - 55 points.

Because she is nominated for State sponsorship by New South Wales she gets a further                          - 5 points.
Her total points score now is                          - 60 points.

Let's look at one last case.

### Frank

Frank is a 35 year old IT professional from London. He has a PHD in renaissance French poetry and has worked as an IT manager for the last 10 years.

Here is how Frank's points score would be calculated.
Because he is aged between 33 and 39 years he gets
- 25 points.
Because he has 8 years experience outside Australia in the past 10 years in an occupation that is in demand he gets
- 15 points.
(These points will be dependant on a successful skills assessment)

His total points score is now                    - 40 points.

Frank has a number of Diplomas in IT but his highest qualification is his PHD so this is the qualification we will use for calculating his points for qualifications and will give him                                   - 20 points.
His total points score is now                    - 60 points.

As you can see from the above the overall points score is made up of the accumulation of each category, and within each category there are possibilities for getting extra points. An extra 5 points here or there can make all the difference so being able to objectively look over your employment history, qualifications and so on to find those extra points is crucial. This is particularly so with the SkillSelect system where eligibility is just the beginning. And yes, I know I said that already but it bears repeating.

So for now, this concludes the votes of the Irish/Australian jury....

# 6 SkillSelect

The SkillSelect system relates to the following visa subclasses only –
457 - Temporary Work (Skilled) - Standard Business Sponsorship
189 - Skilled Independent
190 - Skilled – Nominated
489 - Skilled - Nominated or Sponsored (Provisional)
186 - Employer Nomination Scheme
187 - Regional Sponsored Migration Scheme
132 - Business Talent
188 - Business Innovation and Investment (Provisional)
888 - Business Innovation and Investment (Permanent)
If you don't intend to apply for any of these visa subclasses just move on – nothing to see here.

Still here? Alright then.
When SkillSelect was being introduced in July 2012 I don't mind telling you I was skeptical. The old system was relatively simple; if you had enough points you were eligible to apply for a visa. By comparison SkillSelect sounded like the bureaucratic equivalent of a school dance. If you had enough points you were eligible for admittance

to the dance, but only that. Once in, you had to sit at the side of the dance floor waiting to be asked to dance. So before you even got into the dance hall you had to worry about how attractive you were compared to everyone else who was admitted for that particular dance hour. At least that's what it sounded like in theory.

In hindsight I needn't have worried because SkillSelect has proved to be a substantial improvement on the old system.

Here's how it works and why it's better.

SkillSelect allows skilled workers and business people interested in migrating to Australia to record their details on the SkillSelect system. You do this through what is called an Expression of Interest or E O I for short. This is not to be confused with an E I O, which is only used for the chorus of "Old McDonald had a farm." E I - E I - O.

Joking aside and just to be clear, an EOI is not a visa application, oh no, an EOI is merely an indication that you'd like to be considered for a visa application. The minimum pass mark for an EOI is 60 points. If you don't have 60 points the system won't let you lodge your EOI. A successful lodgment of an EOI means you are now in the dancehall so to speak, but you still have to get asked to dance.

You can understand why I was skeptical.

Once lodged in the SkillSelect system, your EOI is ranked according to your points. This is done by computer and whichever applicants have the most points are invited to apply first. Being eligible is no longer enough, now you must have more points - be more attractive than all the other perspective dancers in the room.

Before you get in a tiz about the state of your frock or the size of your dancing shoes let me reassure you that no one gets to be a wallflower forever because with the SkillSelect system there's a new round of invitations every month. You will go to the ball. Your EOI stays in the system for up to 2 year or until you are invited.

To give you a flavour for what you will need in your EOI here are some of the more common pieces of information required:

Basic personal information, name, address, date of birth etc

- Your nominated occupation.
- Your work experience.
- Your study and education qualifications.
- Your level of English skills.
- Details of a Skills Assessment related to your nominated occupation.
- Your business and investment experience.

**Innovation**

What is truly ground breaking about the SkillSelect system is that for the first time the Department of Immigration has opened the database of prospective applicants to eligible employers and State Governments. This is to help ensure the skilled migration program reflects the economic needs of Australia. It is designed to support the Australian Government in managing who can apply for skilled migration, when they can apply, and in what numbers.

It is also designed to help address regional skill shortages. When you are completing your EOI you can indicate if you are willing to live and work in regional Australia. Employers in regional areas, and State and Territory Governments can use this information to help attract you to their location. This means you can be found and nominated for a visa by an Australian employer, a State Government, a Territory Government, or the Federal Government itself.

The interested parties can't see personal information like your name, date of birth, or other characteristics that could personally identify you. What they can see is your eligibility criteria; that you are an electrician with 10 years experience, for example. They can then get in touch with you anonymously through the system. That's when SkillSelect starts to look more like a dating website than a school dance and therein lies a trap.

As with any dating website the temptation to enhance your attractiveness is strong. Don't do it. The system doesn't take kindly to embellishments, at all. Your invitation to lodge a visa application will be based solely on the information you provide in your EOI. If you lodge a visa application and your points score is less than you claimed in your EOI, your visa will be refused.

There is no fee to submit an EOI to SkillSelect but there is a fee for visa applications and those fees can run to thousands of dollars. If your visa application is refused you won't receive a refund.

### Processing Times

The other brilliant thing about the SkillSelect system is the reduction in processing times. Take the State Sponsored (subclass 190) skilled visa for example; before applicants for this visa can receive an invitation to apply they must apply for sponsorship separately to their State of choice. My experience so far has been that once the State offers sponsorship and updates the applicant's EOI to that effect, the invitation to apply comes through in less than 1 week.

One of my clients received their 190 visa a mere 34 days after lodging their application! Several others have got their visas within 6 weeks. The above examples obviously shouldn't be read as definitive – visa applications can hit road bumps, but SkillSelect has gone a long way towards smoothing that road.

### Business Innovation and Investment Visas

When you submit an EOI for one of these visas, you will be asked to select which State or Territory you wish to live and work in. You can choose one State or Territory, or any State or Territory. If you select only one State or Territory, then only that State or Territory will be able to view your EOI. If you select any State or Territory, then all State or Territory Governments will be able to view your EOI.

This is significant because on a limited basis nominating State or Territory Governments may award additional points towards the innovation points test where they have determined that your proposed business is of exceptional economic benefit to their State or Territory.

If you are nominated by a State or Territory and you have indicated that you meet the points test, you will automatically receive an invitation.

On occasion State and Territory Governments will assess people before they nominate them.

### Strategy

The main strategy for preparing your EOI is to have all the documentation for the visa you are applying for ready before you lodge your EOI. While you don't need to submit documents supporting your claims when you submit your EOI, an invitation to make your visa application may be issued shortly after you submit your

EOI and from that point you will only have 60 days to lodge your complete visa application, which must include all your verified documentation.

For example, if you were applying for a skilled migration visa, the right time to lodge your EOI would be after you have received a positive skill assessment for your occupation and you have an appropriate IELTS test result, if it's required, and you have calculated your points score at 60 points or more.

Depending on the IELTS test score you need, it may take you more than one attempt to get the score you want, and that's even if you are a native English speaker.

Getting a skill assessment can take anything up to 6 months depending on the body you are applying to for the assessment. It's important to have all this done before you lodge your EOI because with the best of intentions you won't be given a chance to verify claims you make in your EOI if you don't have your documentation in place in advance.

# 7 Skill Assessment

"In Australia the plugs are different for electrical appliances."

"Right."

"So if you bring an electrical appliance with an Irish plug to Australia, you're going to need a converter so it will fit Australian sockets."

"That's great. Thanks."

Jim smiled but kept looking at me.

"I think I'm missing something. What has this got to do with my visa?"

"The converter is your skill assessment."

"But I'm a plumber."

"It doesn't make any difference what your profession is, if you're applying for a skilled visa you have to get your skills assessed. That way the Australian Government can see that your qualifications and experience are comparable to Australian standards."

"Right, so where do I go for my converter?"

"Your converter? Now I'm confused."

"For my skill assessment . . . I thought . . . look you started it with the converter," he said making inverted commas in the air with his fingers.

I took a slow deep breath.

"There are various skill assessing bodies in Australia who are authorised to carry out skill assessments for various occupations. If you were a nurse, for example, you would apply through the Australian Nursing and Midwifery Council. If you were an engineer you would apply through Engineers Australia. If you were an IT professional it would be through the Australian Computer Society . . ."

"Plumber, remember."

"Right, in your case it would be through VETASSESS, they handle most of the skills assessment for trades."

"Great, how does that work?"

"The first thing we do is submit your qualifications and experience to VETASSESS. If they're happy with what we send them they will invite you to do a technical interview, which you can do here. We do them all the time. But the . . ."

"What do you know about plumbing?"

I batted my eyelids, "It has something to do with plums right?"

Jim opened his mouth then closed it again.

"You would do the technical interviews here Jim, but it would be with VETASSESS via Skype video. We are a registered VETASSESS technical interview venue. What I was going to say is that because you're a plumber you'll have to do a practical assessment and that is something we don't do here."

"Right, do they have something against plumbers or what?"

"No, it's not just plumbers, electricians and air conditioning/refrigeration mechanics have to do a practical assessment as well."

"Just them?"

"Yes, there are only 3 licensed trades in Australia and those are the ones that have to do a practical assessment."

"Right so where do I go for that?"

"You can go to Belfast or North London."

"What?"

"There's nowhere in the Republic of Ireland where you can do a practical assessment for VETASSESS."

"And how much does it cost?"

"$2,100 AUD."

Jim looked stoically into the distance.

He didn't really but I'll spare you the expletives, reprimands and subsequent apologies that followed. Suffice it to say he didn't take the news well.

"They definitely have it in for plumbers," he said finally.

"No, VETASSESS charge the same for all assessments."

"So you mean the lads who only have to come here and do a Skype interview, they have to pay the full $2,100 AUD too?"

"That's right."

Jim sat back in his chair.

"Well that's alright then. Once the carpenters are paying the same as me that's fine."

### Strategy

Jim went to London a couple of weeks later and completed his practical assessment over the course of a day without a hitch. Even though he had to travel his skills were relatively easy to get assessed.

The list of all occupations eligible for skilled migration to Australia is called the Consolidated Sponsored Occupation List or CSOL for short. If you can't find your occupation on CSOL look for occupations on the list that sound like they might be close to what you do. For example, Building Surveyor is not on the CSOL, but Building Inspector is.

To find out if an occupation on the CSOL is the same as your occupation but with a different name, you will need to go to the source, the basis from which all the assessing bodies take their guidance and that, surprisingly, is the Australian Bureau of Statistics. In their rounding up and categorizing of the population of Australia the Bureau of Statistics developed the Australian and New Zealand Standard Classification of Occupations list or ANZSCO list for short. You can find the full ANZSCO list on the Australian Bureau of Statistics website.

Here's an example of how you can use it. I had a client who was a Professional Auctioneer with many years of experience. When she looked on the CSOL, Professional Auctioneer was not on the list. From experience I knew there was a similar profession to Professional Auctioneer on the CSOL but it had a different name – Land Economist. We consulted the ANZSCO list and found that the tasks, duties and requisite qualifications for a Land Economist, which was on the CSOL at the time, were very similar to a professional auctioneer. My client was able to get assessed as a land economist and we proceeded with her skilled visa application from there.

While skill assessment is the first step for the skilled migration visa application process, it may also be a requirement for employer sponsored migration visa categories depending on your occupation and nationality.

# 8 State Sponsorship

"Have you considered Murwillumbah?"

"What's that?"

"It's a town in northern New South Wales. It's near the border with Queensland."

"Considering I'd never heard of it till you just said it now and considering I have my heart set on Sydney, eh, no, I hadn't considered MurryLumbar."

"Well I think you're going to have to consider Murwillumbah or somewhere similar because you don't have the points to go to Sydney."

Deirdre sat up straight in her chair.

"I-am-not-short."

"Pardon?"

"You just said I was short for Sydney."

"Em, no, I didn't. I said you didn't have enough points to go to Sydney."

"My height doesn't affect my ability to do my work you know. My clients say I'm an excellent hair stylist."

"I'm sure you are Deirdre, but you're still short, I mean, you still don't have enough points to apply for a skilled independent visa."

"So it's not a height thing?"

"No."

"Why can't I go to Sydney then?"

"Because in order to apply for a skilled independent visa you need 60 points. You only have 50. You could try and get sponsored by an employer in Sydney but from what you've told me you don't want to do that."

"No way, I want to be free. I don't want to be tied to anyone."

"Fine. So your next option would be to apply for a regional sponsored migration visa, subclass 489."

Deirdre was up and pacing, "Good. Good. I like the sound of that."

"O-kay, but that would mean that you have to live and work in a regional part of the State you apply to."

"Okay. . . With you . . . We're sort of work-shopping the problem here, I get it."

"You want to go to Sydney which is in New South Wales, so I'm suggesting somewhere in regional New South Wales, which would be Murwillumbah."

"Okay, so that's, like, a suburb in Sydney. I could do that."

"No, Murwillumbah is a small town."

"Even better."

"It's not a suburb of Sydney though, it's . . ."

"A little bit out of town. That could work too."

"It's 800 kilometers out of town."

"What?"

"Murwillumbah is 800 kilometers from Sydney."

"Well that's not going to work, I'd never manage that commute."

"Deirdre, regional means regional, it has to be outside Sydney and you have to live there, you couldn't live in Sydney and commute, even if the distance wasn't prohibitive."

"But 800 kilometers, isn't there somewhere a bit closer?"

"Well yes, there are many towns closer but the

conditions still apply, you must live and work in the region."

Deirdre flopped back in her chair.

"I'm a city girl Mege. I want to be where the action is. I don't want to be stuck in Woop Woop."

"You know Woop Woop's not a real place, right?"

"Sure it is, it's right next door to, Waga Waga," she said waging her head like a dog.

"No Waga Waga is a real place. It's actually in regional New South Wales."

"You're joking."

"No, I'm serious. It's at the other end of the State and it's a bit closer to Sydney by about 350 kilometers."

"That's just great, only 450 kilometers from Sydney," Deirdre said standing up again, "my Australian dream was living in the bright lights and golden beaches of Sydney, not spending the rest of my days in Waga Waga with 3 other people and a dog."

"Well the first thing about regional State sponsorship is you only have to live in the area for 2 years."

"Oh," said Deirdre sitting down again and leaning in, "go on."

"The other thing is that Waga Waga has a population of 47,000 people, so, while it's not Sydney, it's not a small, small town, if you know what I mean."

"I think I do."

"I suggest you have a think about what we've talked about today and do some research. There are plenty of great towns and small cities in regional Australia and I'm sure you will find one you like and would be happy to live in for 2 years. After that you will be free to go and live in Sydney."

"Right! Look out Google here I come."

Deirdre's case is not that uncommon, many people only think of large cities like Sydney, Melbourne, Perth and Brisbane when they are considering moving to Australia but life in a small town in Australia can be very pleasant. I went to school in a town called Armidale and I have vey fond memories of it. Small towns in Australia have a particular charm to them and they're not all inland. The popular Australian TV soap, "Home and Away," is set in a fictional town called Summer Bay which could very easily be a coastal town in regional New South Wales.

### Subclass 489 and 190
The 10 points highlighted in Deirdre's case are for regional State sponsorship - Subclass 489. You can also get sponsored by a State without the regional restriction - Subclass 190, but there are only 5 points allocated for this subclass. You have to live in the State for 2 years with this subclass also. The State Governments set this condition as a payoff for sponsoring you.

### Occupation matters
Your occupation plays a part in State sponsorship too. State and regional sponsorship are driven by labour shortages so you also need to have an occupation that is in demand in the State you are considering for sponsorship. Each State Government chooses what occupations they would like to sponsor depending on the needs of their State labour market and economy. Like the Federal Government each State Government has a list of occupations in demand for their State. This is not to be confused with the CSOL, which is the list of occupations relevant to migration for the whole of Australia.

How it works.
When you submit your EOI for a skilled migration visa in the SkillSelect system you indicate what State you are applying for sponsorship to. Your actual application for State sponsorship can then be made after you've submitted your EOI.

State Governments review your EOI by accessing it through the SkillSelect system after they have received your application for State sponsorship. All going well once the State Government in question approves your sponsorship, they log into your EOI in the SkillSelect system and indicate that they have sponsored you. The Department of Immigration will then generate an invitation to apply which will be sent to you or your appointed migration agent.

Deirdre bustled back into my office a few weeks later to let me know how her research had gone.

"You'll never guess what's happened Mege. I'm going to live in Tamworth."

"That's great Deirdre. Tamworth is a lovely town. What decided it for you?"

"My Daddy. He was over for tea last Thursday and I was going on about how my head was spinning with the names of all these little towns in Australia like, Wagga Wagga, and Bombala, and Dubbo, and Mudgee, and then I said Tamworth and that's when it happened, " she put her hand on her heart, " he came over all emotional. He said if his little girl had to live in Australia, Tamworth would be the place he would choose."

"That's nice."

"Nice! I couldn't believe it Mege. He said if I lived in Tamworth he'd love to come to visit his little girl there."

I should point out that Deirdre was 35 years old.

"He'd never said anything like that about Sydney, Mege; the opposite in fact. The way he used to talk about Australia you'd think I was going to live on Mars."

"He must like Country and Western then?"

Deirdre was about to make another point and had raised a finger for emphasis, "He what?"

"Your father must like Country and Western music?"

"He loves it. He lives it in fact; cowboy boots, string ties, the lot. Down our way they call him Tex. What's that got to do with Tamworth?"

"Tamworth is the Country and Western music capital of Australia. The Tamworth Country Music Festival happens every year and it's the biggest festival of its kind in the Southern Hemisphere."

Deirdre wasn't looking at me anymore though her finger was still poised midair. "The Tamworth Country Music Festival," I went on, "is the second biggest country music festival in the world. I know because I used to go to school in Armidale which is close to Tamworth and we used to go on field trips when the festival was on. I can remember. . ."

"The crafty oul fecker!" Deirdre said tapping the side of her nose with her finger, "he knew. . ."

"Pardon?"

"My Dad. I wondered why he was taking the whole regional Australia thing so well. He even suggested staying in New South Wales. 'At least you'll be in the same State as Sydney,' he said."

"Tamworth is a big town Deirdre; the population is around 47,000."

"I'm sure it's great," she chuckled, "well at least the oul fecker will come and visit me if I'm there.

"At least once ever year."

"For the festival," we both said together.

# 9 English Language test  — IELTS.

"It's not personal Philip, it's just a requirement for your visa application."

"But I am a British citizen, that should be sufficient."

"It can't be biased Philip, the same rule applies to all applicants for your visa regardless of which passport they hold."

"Surely Australia, as a former colony, should show a little respect for it's former . . . I mean the Queen is still the head of State down there isn't she?"

"She is Philip, but she doesn't affect the requirements for your visa. Every applicant must provide an IELTS test result."

"Well I think it's ridiculous; particularly for an Englishman."

"Be that as it may you will still have to take the test if you want to apply for this visa."

"Fine, fine, send me the details and I'll take the silly test."

"I suggest you do some preparation for the test. There is an excellent website called. . ."

"Thank you for your suggestion and while I value your expertise in matters legal I think a simple English test will be well within my grasp."

"That's the thing Philip, it's not simple, I've had a number of clients who needed to retake the test because. ."

"These would be Irish clients, yes?"

"Well the majority of them were but . . ."

"Say no more Megan, I'll be in touch with my results forthwith. Good day to you."

"My name isn't . . . ," I started but he was gone.

## Testing English Proficiency

There are two approved English proficiency tests for migration purposes, the Occupation English Test or OET for short, and the more common and preferred International English Language Testing System or IELTS for short. The IELTS test is conducted on a worldwide basis by the British Council and has 4 separate components you are tested on –
- Reading
- Writing
- Listening
- Speaking

The test takes about 3 hours and is designed to test your English proficiency in everyday workplace and social situations.

## Score

You are scored in each component from 0 to 9. Your score in each component is then added together and averaged to give you an overall score.

For example if you scored –
- Reading  - 5
- Writing  - 4
- Listening - 8
- Speaking  - 7

Your overall score would be
$5 + 4 + 8 + 7 = 24 \div 4 = $ **6**

Your overall score will fall within one of 9 bands laid out by the British Council; 9 being "Expert," and 0 being "Non User," or basically no English language ability at all.

The Immigration Department is only interested in the 6th band or higher. Also, they're not interested in your overall score; they want to know your individual component scores. And lastly, just to make it a little more complicated, they have created their own classification system for your IELTS score -
- Superior
- Proficient
- Competent

I'm telling you this so you don't get confused between the British Council band names and the Department of Immigration classifications system. Needless to say it is the Department of Immigration's classification system that counts when it comes to your visa application.

Here are the requirements for the different classifications and how many points are allocated for each-

**Superior**
You need to score 8 in each of the 4 components; reading, writing, listening and speaking.

A classification of Superior = 20 points

**Proficient**
You need to score 7 in each of the 4 components; reading, writing, listening and speaking.

A classification of Proficient = 10 Points

**Competent**
You need to score 6 in each of the 4 components; reading,

writing, listening and speaking.

A classification of Competent = 0 Points.
(While it receives no points a "competent" score is a basic requirement for all Skilled Migration points based visas.)

### Preparation

It is important to prepare for the test before you take it to give yourself the best chance of achieving the score you want. Past test papers and reading books are available on the IELTS website –
www.ielts.org

### Fee

The IELTS test fee in Ireland is €185 and £140 in the U.K. You should book your test well in advance as some test centers only offer the test once a month.

### Phillip

I didn't hear from Philip for 3 months, which was a bit unusual because normally it takes between 4 to 6 weeks to sit the IELTS test and get a result. When he did finally send me his IELTS test results he had a classification of "Competent," which means he scored 6 in each of the 4 components; reading, writing, listening and speaking. With a classification of competent he still had the minimum pass mark, which was sufficient for his visa application, and we went ahead with his application.

Considering how gung-ho he was about the test I suspect the delay in sending in his test results was because he had to retake the test at least once, if not twice, though he never admitted this to me of course.

# 10 Medicals

"I really want to go to Australia and everything, but I don't want to go through the obstacle course."

"I understand Bernie, but that's what I'm here for, to help you navigate the different forms, document check lists, lodgments dates, skill assessment criteria, and so on. I know it can look daunting but I've helped hundreds of people through this process and I'm sure you'll be fine."

Bernie shifted in his chair, "That's great Mege, but I still don't want to go through the obstacle course."

"I see. That could be a problem Bernie, because there really isn't any other way to get your visa. Maybe rather than thinking of it as an obstacle course you could think of it as a series of steps you need to take. A form here, a certificate there."

"I'm grand with all the paperwork, the forms, the lodgments, everything. I'm just not doing the obstacle course."

I put my pen down, "Your talking about a real obstacle course, aren't you."

"Yeah, what were you talking about?"

"I was talking about the metaphoric obstacle course."

"Well I'm not doing that one either. I'm not doing any

obstacle course," he shifted in his chair again, "I know I'm fat and everything, but they shouldn't hold that against me."

I held up my hand, "There is no obstacle course Bernie."

"There isn't? What about the medicals? I thought there was an obstacle course for the medicals, because I smoke you know, I might as well get that out here and now."

I held up my other hand, "You're not joining the marines Bernie; the medicals have nothing to with fitness, in that sense."

"Oh."

"The medical checks are primarily there for two reasons. Firstly, to make sure you don't have a contagious condition that would be harmful to the Australian public. They particularly want to check for tuberculosis."

"Fair enough."

"The second reason is to check that you don't have a condition that could end up costing the Australian taxpayer a lot of money to provide health care for, or put such a demand on the health care system that it could lead to Australian citizens being denied access to health care services that are in short supply, like a heart transplant, for example."

"Right, well that sounds reasonable," he shifted in his chair again, "So it will be on a treadmill then with the oxygen mask and all that?"

"Pardon?"

"For the medical checks, it'll be the treadmill and the oxygen mask and all that?"

"No, it's basically a chest x-ray and a blood test."

"And that's it."

"That's it."

"So I just go along to my GP and get him to organize that?"

"No, you have to go to a special Doctor that is

approved by the Australian Government, they are called panel Doctors. There is a list of them on the Department of Immigration website. They will send the results of your medical check directly to the Department of Immigration."

"Well that's great then." Bernie looked left and right then leaned in, "And there won't be a problem with the smoking?"

"Well it depends on what brand you smoke."

"Really!!"

"No Bernie, I'm teasing, whether you smoke or not has nothing to do with the medical checks."

"Great. Speaking of smoking . . . are we finished here for now?"

### Other Considerations.

All family members included in the visa application have to have medical checks.

If you have dependants who are not migrating with you, they must also have a medical check. The reason for this is the Department of Immigration wants to know if anyone has a serious medical condition regardless and if they do this could cause an issue. Failing a medical normally leads to a visa refusal overall even if the main applicant is healthy and passes their medical check. The most common occurrence of this is a dependent who may be a "non-migrating" child from a previous relationship or marriage.

Applicants under 11 years of age don't have to have the chest x-ray or HIV blood test, instead they are given a full medical examination.

A worldwide list of panel Doctors is available at www.imm.gov.au/contact/panel-doctors

In Ireland panel doctors are located in Dublin and Cork, and currently charge –

- €270 per adult applicant
- €255 per child (aged between 11-15)
- €70 per child (under 11)

Applicants are responsible for all costs associated with the medical examinations.

## Strategy
The main strategy is wait until you are asked. Undertake your medical checks when you are officially requested to do so by the case officer from the Department of Immigration.

## *11 Police clearances*

"It was a long time ago. I was young and stupid. I've cleaned up my life since then; got myself on track."

"That's great Frank, what exactly were the charges?"

"Drugs."

"What about drugs?"

"They were drug charges."

"Right, so you don't know what the charges were exactly."

"I just told you they were drug charges."

"I see, so you were arrested for bringing small planes filled with cocaine into the country from Columbia?"

"God no. I was caught with a bit of pot in the 80's."

"So you're not a major drug Baron?"

"Very funny. Look this is my life we're talking about here."

"I'm sorry Frank, you're quite right. It's just that if I had a penny for every person who was caught with a bit of pot in the 80's and thought it was going to derail their chances of a visa for Australia I'd be a rich woman."

"Really, with all those "pennies.""

"True. Maybe if I added the pennies from all the people who thought a speeding ticket was going to derail their visa chances . . ."

"So you're basically saying we don't need to mention my drug charges?"

"No, we will disclose them of course, but first we need to find out what the charges were specifically, and then what has been noted on your record and when."

"Right, and that's what the police clearance is all about."

"Fundamentally the police clearance has to do with character; whether you are of good character to be specific. The general idea is that before granting a visa, the Department of Immigration wants to check that the person they are about to give the visa to is of good character. To help them make this evaluation they enlist the help of the local constabulary in the country the potential migrant is currently living. The local Police check back through their database to see if you have any criminal convictions or anything else on your criminal record."

"So the local Police for me would be the UK Police?"

"Have you lived in the UK for the last ten years?"

"Yes."

"Have you lived in any other country for more than a year in the last ten years?"

"Other than the UK?"

"Yes."

"Well, apart from the 3 years I spent in Columbia establishing my drug cartel, no."

"I see. Well we're going to need to get a Police clearance certificate from the Columbian Police for those 3 years. Is that going to be a problem Frank?"

"It's depressing how easily you see me as a drug Baron."

"What can I say Frank, it's just a vibe you give out."

"Very funny, no I didn't live in Columbia. I've never even been to Columbia."

"Sure you haven't Frank. I believe you, honest."

"I'm going to ignore that. I did live in Germany for 18 months about 3 years ago."

"Right, well joking aside we will need to get a Police clearance from the German Police for that period. The official name for a Police clearance certificate varies from country to country. The German document we want is called a Police Good Conduct Certificate and it costs €13. You can apply for it through your local German embassy."

"And in the UK?"

"For the UK the document we want is called an ACPO Police Certificate and it costs £35. It's issued by The Association of Chief Police Officers, or ACPO, for short, and you can download the application form on their website."

### Strategy

The strategy for the Police clearance is the same as for the medical checks - wait until you are asked. Normally you would apply for a Police clearance when you are officially requested to do so by the case officer from the Department of Immigration.

### Other Considerations

For immigration purposes a Police certificate is deemed to be valid for 12 months from the issue date.

For Ireland the relevant document is called a Police Certificate of Character. You apply for it in person to your local Garda station. There is no charge.

MEGE DALTON

# Section 3    Visas

## 12 Skilled Independent Visa

James looked at me earnestly, "I'm very interested in learning how to surf and I really like kangaroos."

"I see. Have you ever seen a kangaroo?"

"Yes, in the Zoo but I think the kangaroos in Australia are much bigger."

"Possibly, the red kangaroos can get quite big."

"I'd like to meet one but I'm a bit afraid . . ." he looked over his shoulder as if to check there wasn't a kangaroo standing behind him, "I'm afraid they would be much bigger than me."

"I see."

James was six years old. He had accompanied his father Alan to my office for an initial consultation about Alan's visa options.

"Well, if you see a red kangaroo . . ." I said.

"Yes."

". . . and it's really big; much bigger than you. . ."

"Yes."

"You can stand behind your Dad here and nothing will happen you."

James looked very relieved. His Dad, Alan, not so much, worried would be a better description, "Thanks Mege," he said.

"Anytime Alan. If you want any more tips on bush craft just ask."

James had been eyeing a toy kangaroo on my desk. Alan picked it up and asking permission with a nod of his head in James's direction said, "You're all heart."

I nodded approval and we both watched James skip off to the corner of the office to play. Alan turned back to me, "So you reckon I don't need to get sponsored then?"

"No I don't think you need to. You're a carpenter, which is on Schedule 1 of CSOL which means you don't have to get state sponsorship."

"What's seesaw?"

"CSOL is the list of all occupations eligible for skilled migration to Australia. You're under 35 years of age, so that's in your favor too, and you have more than a competent level of English. That all adds up to a good application for a skilled independent visa."

"And that's better than being sponsored?"

"Well it gives you more choices. In particular, you are free to live and work wherever you like in Australia.

"That sounds deadly," Alan said ruffling James's hair as he went past, "How do I get started?"

"The first thing we have to do is get your skills assessed. You're a bricklayer so that would be with VETASSESS. You can do a technical interview here via Skype video."

"Grand, how much will that cost?"

"VETASSESS charge $2,100 AUD for skill assessments."

Alan whistled. Without turning around James threw his head back and whistled too.

"While your skill assessment is in process you will need to do an IELTS test."

"What's that for?"

"Your English language ability."

"Ah here. I've never been that great at writing essays or spelling and that. . ."

"I could help you with spelling Daddy," James said, "Button.  B – U – T – T – O – N."

"That's great mate," said Alan ruffling James hair again.

"The IELTS test is a requirement of the visa."

"Do I have to pay for that?"

"Yes, the cost is €185 on average."

"Right, well we'll give it a shot, won't we Jimbo."

"Yes Daddy," said James.

"Once we get your skill assessment back," I continued, "and your IELTS test scores, we can lodge your Expression of Interest or EOI."

"My what?"

"It's the first part of the process.  In essence you will be letting the Australian Government know that you're interested in migrating to Australia."

"Grand."

"Then we will wait for an invitation to apply.  Once that comes through we can put your visa application together and lodge it, then while it is processing we will get you to do your medicals and organise your Police clearances."

"How much is all that going to cost?"

"There is no application fee for the expression of interest."

"Deadly."

"The application cost for the visa application on the other hand is expensive.  It is $3,060 AUD for yourself as the main applicant. . ."

Alan started to whistle again.

". . . it will be $1,530 AUD for your wife. . ."

James joined in whistling.

". . . and  $765 AUD for James here.  Do you have any other children?"

"No, and at that those prices, we're not going to until

we're in Australia."

"There is no charge for Police clearances and the medicals will be €270 each for yourself and your wife," turning to James I asked, "How old are you James?"

"I'm 6 and three quarters."

"Very good," turning back to Alan I said, "and it will be €70 for James's medical. It would be €255 if he was aged between 11 and 15."

Alan cocked his head to one side while he did some mental calculations, "So I'm looking at the guts of four and a half grand in application fees."

"That's sounds about right."

Alan looked to the left as if to an unseen camera and said, "Well considering how much I am expending on application fees I would be foolhardy not to invest the relatively small fee you charge to ensure my application is successful and in so doing protect the capital I expend on my application fees."

". . . eh, yes Alan, I couldn't have said it better myself."

"So what's the story once we lodge the application?" Alan asked.

"Then we wait for approval."

"How long do you reckon?"

"It can vary but at the moment Skilled Independent visas are processing in about 3 months."

"That's brilliant. So when would we have to go?"

"Once your visa is granted you normally have about 8 months to activate it?"

"How do I do that?

"All you have to do is enter Australia."

"That's great Mege," Alan said, then turning to James, "Then we'll be down under mate, what?"

"Down under what Daddy?"

"I'll explain on the way out Jimbo."

"Okay Daddy."

## *13 Employer Sponsored Visas*

Bill was on the phone from Toowoomba, a mid sized town north of Brisbane in Queensland.

"My mate in the RSL club told me about you and how you fixed him up with a barber."

"I see. Is that 'Happy Snips' on James Street?"

"That's the one."

"Yes, I think I know the client you're talking about."

"Well I need you to do the same for me."

"You're looking to hire a barber?"

"No, not a barber, an upholsterer. We run an upholstery shop."

"It's funny you should be looking for an upholsterer, because I did a visa assessment for an upholsterer only last week."

"Ripper! Would he like to come and work in the Garden City?"

"What makes you think it's a man Bill?"

"Well I just . . ."

"I'm teasing you Bill, it is a man, and he was open to working in regional Australia. I'll have to get in touch with him and see if he is interested."

"Beauty."

"Have you sponsored someone before Bill?"

"No, this will be our first time."

"Okay, the first thing we need to do is prepare your application to become a business sponsor."

"Fair enough. What does that entail?"

"You need to show you are a lawfully operating business. You also need to show you have a record of employing local labour and that you have non-discriminatory work practices. You will need to meet the Australian Government's training requirements and pay the market salary rate for the position you're interested in sponsoring."

"That doesn't sound too hard."

"Good. Can you send me some information about your business?"

"What kind of info would you like?"

"Your website, e-brochures that kind of thing. Something I can show my client to give him a feel for your business. Can you also send me a description of the position you would like him to fill and what you intend to pay. I will pass it all on to my client and if he likes what he sees I'll forward you his details and set up an interview with you."

"An interview! I think I should at least talk to the bloke on the phone before he flies over here for an interview."

"We would conduct the interview on Skype video Bill."

"Oh, right-o, Skype. Sounds good."

I finished my call with Bill and within an hour I was on the phone with Dermot, the upholsterer I had assessed the previous week.

"Toowoonga?" he said, "Where's that?"

"It's ToowooMBa Dermot and it's in Queensland."

"Which end of Queensland? That place is huge."

"It's about a 2 hour drive north west of Brisbane."

"And they're looking for an upholsterer?"

"Yes, very much so."

"Right, so what would I have to do?"

"I'll send you some information on Bill's company so you can see if it looks like the sort of place you'd like to work. Do some research yourself on Toowoomba itself to see if you would like to live there. Check house rental prices and have a look at the kind of schools they have and what the amenities are like. I've been to Toowoomba many times and I can tell you that it's a lovely country town but you do your own research and decide for yourself."

"Right, will do."

"You'll need to send me your CV and any pictures you have of your work. Also, if you can make a quick video of your work over the weekend that would be ideal."

"A video? How would I do that?"

"Other clients I've suggested this to have just used their mobile phones and then uploaded the video to YouTube."

"Oh right."

"It's a simple thing but it can make a big difference to a prospective employer because they can see you in action doing the work they're interested in hiring you for."

"I'll have a go over the weekend. The wife's brother is very good at that sort of thing so I'll get him to give me a hand."

"Great. Then if Toowoomba and Bill's company are of interest to you, and if Bill likes your CV and video, I'll set up a time for you to do a Skype video interview with Bill."

"Grand."

"If you're both happy to go ahead, we can begin to prepare the sponsorship, nomination and visa applications. They are then all lodged together."

"And that's for permanent residency?"

"No, this is for temporary residence. The visa is a standard business sponsorship visa subclass 457. It is classed temporary (Long Stay) and lasts for 4 years."

"And what do I do after the 4 years?"

"You can use the temporary visa as a means of getting permanent residency. Once you've been working with Bill for at least 2 years I would recommend that he can sponsor you through for permanent residency"

"Okay, sounds like a plan. Now, what kind of visa do I have to get for my wife and kids?"

"Your family are included in your visa application. They will have to get the medical checks and Police clearances the same as you but once the visa is granted you each have a visa in your own names."

Dermot was silent for a moment.

"What happens if Bill turns out to be a terrible boss, can I go and work for someone else?"

"Yes you can. You won't need a new visa if it's still valid but it will be the same arrangement again; you would need to find a new employer who is an approved sponsor."

"Fair enough."

Dermot went on to do his research on Toowoomba and he really liked it. He made a great little video of his work the following week and Bill loved it. Their Skype video interview went so well it ended up like a mutual appreciation society meeting.

2 months later Dermot and his family had relocated to Toowoomba where they have been ever since. Bill went on to tell his other "mates" about his new Irish employee and I've helped a number of them do something similar since.

Bill and Dermot's story highlights the most standard type of employer sponsored visa which is the subclass 457. There are other employer sponsored subclasses including labour agreements which facilitate sponsorship on a large scale. Labour agreements are particularly popular in the mining industry for example.

Regardless of the employer sponsored visa subclass, the component parts are the same as Bill and Dermot's story. The employer needs to be approved as a sponsor. They need to nominate the prospective employee and the prospective employee applies for the visa. There are varying requirements to do with health insurance and English language ability which change depending on what passport you hold.

Employer sponsored visas are a great way to live and work in Australia and are an excellent stepping stone to permanent residency if used strategically.

# 14 Working Holiday Visa

"The only thing I'm sure of is I want to get out of here," Jimmy laughed as he necked his pint of Guinness. We were chatting at a social event and the subject of migrating to Australia had come up. Jimmy was like many young people I've talked to in Ireland; not sure what country they want to go to, but sure they want to get out.

"Some of my mates are in Perth," he said, "but I don't know if Australia's for me."

"Get yourself a working holiday visa young man." I said a little Guinnessed up myself, "Go and find out for yourself; maybe you'll love it."

"A working holiday visa?"

"Most definitely. It's the young person's visa of choice. A working holiday visa is Australia's way of saying to the rest of the world, 'We're sexy and we know it.'"

Jimmy splurted his pint laughing.

"How do you mean?"

"Tourists usually visit a country for 2 weeks at the most, and while on holiday they're not expected to contribute to the community beyond what they spend, which the holiday country usually tries to help them do in excess. Well, Jimmy, in Australia we do things differently.

We don't mess around. We get our tourists to stay for at least a year and not only that we put them to work. We get our tourists to contribute to the community by putting all the money they earn back into the economy, and the best part is they're grateful to do it. For young people curious about Australia but with no definite plans to move there, the working holiday visa is the one I recommend, and the best part is it's relatively easy to get."

"Sure it is, what do you charge for it?"

"Why, not a penny young man. You don't need a migration agent like me to get a working holiday visa because it's a fairly simple process to apply for it online."

"Oh."

Jimmy looked more than a little disappointed I wasn't going to try and "sell" him. I didn't want to confuse him with too much information but looked at another way the working holiday visa is also a try-before-you-buy visa. It gives people a chance to see the country, get experience of what it is like to live and work in Australia, and see if it is somewhere they might like to settle.

### Eligibility

For the working holiday visa you need to be between 18 and 30 years of age. You also need to be a citizen of one of the countries on the list below and lastly you need to have $5,000 AUD in your bank account.

- Belgium
- Canada
- Cyprus
- Denmark
- Estonia
- Finland
- France
- Germany
- Ireland

- Italy
- Japan
- Korea
- Malta
- Netherlands
- Norway

The working holiday visa is valid for 12 months. The Australian Government want people to take the holiday part seriously so they insist you move around. One of the conditions of the visa is that you can't work for the same employer for more than 6 months.

You can study on this visa but only for 4 months.

It is possible to extend this visa to a second year but to be eligible to do this you have to work in regional Australia for 3 months during your first year visa.

### Strategy

The working holiday visa can be a stepping-stone visa. If your overall goal is a permanent residency visa you can use the working holiday visa to get you to Australia and once there you can apply to work with the kind of employers you would like to work for permanently. You can use your temporary employment as a demonstration of your talents, skills and abilities. If your employer wants to hire you they can apply for a 457 visa for you. Once the 457 is lodged you can apply to Government to be allowed to go back to work for the same employer.

This kind of thing is happening everyday in Australia, people with the right qualifications and experience on working holiday visas are being snapped up by employers and put on 457 visas.

Also a working holiday allows you to remain onshore if

you are lodging a skilled migration visa. This means you don't have the extra cost of having to fly out of Australia to lodge your application and then fly back in.

It is a good strategy to organize the 3 months regional work early in the first 12 months of the working holiday visa. Whether you know if you want to stay for 2 years or not, getting the 3 months regional work out of the way gives you the option. If you leave it too late to organize your regional work you may not be able to find a suitable employer in a suitable region and you could end up in work you would prefer not to be doing, in a place you would prefer not to be doing it in. Remember Australia is a huge country.

### Stay Legit
This visa is one of the more common visas that people overstay on. Don't.

I suspect this happens through negligence rather than intent but the Migration Department takes a very dim view of overstaying. If you overstay any visa you become illegal and when you finally leave the country you will be subject to a 3 year re-entry ban.

# 15 Spouse Visas

"I just love her soo much." Andy delivered this conversation stopper with glistening eyes and a vice grip lock on his fiancé's hand. Agnuska smiled awkwardly and looked around the room for something to change the subject.

She and Andy had met in Ireland a year before and now Andy wanted to bring her back to Adelaide to get married. She was very keen on the idea and up to this point in our initial meeting had been very involved, that was until Andy started gushing. Uncharacteristic for an Aussie man, his display of emotion was obviously disturbing her eastern European reserve.

"So the main thing you will need is proof of your relationship," I said, hoping to bring Andy back to the point at hand.

"We're getting married," he replied, "isn't that enough?"

"No, in order to get Agnuska a spouse visa you will need to demonstrate that you've been in a long term, committed relationship for at least 12 months or more."

"Oh."

"How do we demonstrate?" Agnuska asked.

"Well, as it stands your relationship would be considered de facto which the Department of Immigration recognizes as having the same standing as a lawfully married couple, so you would need demonstrate that you've been in a de facto relationship as a couple for at least 12 months. For example, if you've been living together for the last 12 months."

"So no need to be married?" Agnuska asked.

Andy inhaled sharply and looked at the ceiling.

"Not from the immigration departments perspective," I continued - carefully, "They recognize a de facto relationships the same as a marriage. It's similar to the way they recognise same sex marriages as being the same as opposite sex marriages, or de facto same sex relationships."

"Oh, the gays too?" Agnuska said.

"Look of course we're getting married." Andy interrupted.

"But we don't have to?" Agnuska replied, looking to me for confirmation. I smiled at them in what I hoped was a reassuring and calming way, "Whether you get married or not is for you to decide. From the Immigration Department's perspective the main point is that you can show you are in a de facto relationship with each other for 12 months or more. To do that you need . . ."

Agnuska sat bolt upright, "We're screwing."

I looked at her blankly.

"Screwed," Andy corrected, "We're screwed."

I looked at them both, relieved but confused, and hoping one of them would explain what they were talking about.

"You said we had to demonstrate 12 months of living together, right?" asked Andy.

"Yes."

"Well we've only been living together for 9 months."

"Can you prove that?"

"Eh…"

"What kind of proof?" Agnuska asked.

"Do you own the property you live in or do you rent?"

"We rent," said Andy.

"Are both your names on the lease?"

"Yes," said Andy, "we got a new place when we moved in together."

"That's great," I said, "having both your names on the lease is really good evidence. Often people move in together but don't put the new partner's name on the lease or mortgage. Are the utility bills in both your names too?"

"Yes."

"That's great too and pretty much covers all the official forms of proof we need. The next kind of evidence we need is proof of your ongoing relationship. This would be photos of you together at different functions, at different times. Any trips you might have taken together, particularly anything that has both your names on it like air tickets or hotel reservations."

"We should be able to get that."

"Great. We also may need to get statutory declarations from your friends and family stating the nature and length of your relationship. That would include the Australian side of the family Andy."

"What is a statutory declaration?" Agnuska asked.

"It's a written sworn statement of fact that is witnessed and notarised," I replied.

"That shouldn't be a problem either," said Andy, "but what are we going to do about the nine months?"

"We're in January now," I said, "so you will be able to demonstrate 12 months in April. We can make your application then. Current processing time is 8-9 months at the Australian high commission in London, which is where the application is lodged if you're based in Ireland."

"And then that's it?"

"No, there is a second stage to the visa process."

"Oh for crying out loud!" Andy threw his hands in the air.

"The second stage of the visa is relatively straight forward. It involves another application process which includes evidence that your de facto relationship is still ongoing."

"When do we make this second application?" asked Agnuska.

"You make it on the 2 year anniversary of your application. So if we lodge your application in April you will make the second stage application in April 2 years hence."

"Hens?"

"2 years from this April. Once the second stage is approved you will be issued with permanent residency."

Andy, who had been looking at the ceiling, as if for guidance, lurched back into the conversation, "Permanent residency? So she'll always be a second class citizen?"

"No, on both counts," I replied, "She won't be an Australian citizen at all. That is a process she can go through once she has been a permanent resident and meets the citizen requirements. (See chapter 21 Citizenship.) But being a permanent resident is almost the same as being a citizen. The main difference is that permanent residents can't vote in Australian elections or run for public office but other than that they have equal standing in the community."

"Is a permanent resident an Australian?" Agnuska asked.

"Technically no. You're not an Australian until you become a citizen."

"But I can in time, right?"

"Yes, once you have your permanent residency and you meet the citizenship requirements."

"Then I'll be an Australian," Agnuska said turning to Andy, "Just like you Andy Pandy."

The sun rose in Andy's face as he beamed back at her.

6 months later an email arrived in my inbox from Agnuska and Andy with a wedding photo attached. A year after that I got another email with a photo of their new baby girl whom they named Mege.

Okay I made that last part up. They called their little girl Natasha but it's the thought that counts, no?

### Other considerations

Andy and Agnuska's story is an example of an Off Shore Temporary Spouse visa Subclass 309. It is the provisional subclass because they had only 12 months proof of their relationship. If you are in a spousal relationship for 3 years or more you are entitled to apply for the Permanent Spouse visa Subclass 100. There is no second stage application for this visa subclass as you go straight to permanent residency.

## 16 Family Visas

Ethel was sixty-two and sick of Skype. She had three children living in Australia and was tired of watching her grandkids grow up through a halting video chat window. Her children had already been in touch with me from Australia, and Ethel and I were now meeting in my offices in Dublin. She spread her hands on the table and leaned back in her chair, "What are my options?"

"Well the first thing we need to figure out is if you meet the "balance of family" requirement?"

Ethel said nothing, waiting for me to explain.

"How many children do you have in total?"

"Five."

"And how many live in Australia?"

"My two boys and one of my girls."

"So three altogether. Are they all permanent residents?"

"No, they all have citizenship."

"Good, that's even better. The balance of family requirement States that at least half of your children must be living in Australia permanently, without meeting that requirement you wouldn't be able to apply for any of the parent visas."

"There's more than one parent visa?"

"Yes, and which one you apply for depends on how much money you have at your disposal and how much time you're willing to wait. For example, if you apply for a Parent visa, subclass 103, there is a cap on the number of these visas issued each year so your application would go in a queue. There could be 20,000+ applications in the queue at any given time which makes for a very long wait."

"How long?"

"Between 8 to 10 years."

Ethel looked down at her extended fingernails, "Next."

"I wouldn't dismiss that subclass just yet. There is a strategy we can use with it that I'll come back to when we've explored your other options."

"Okay."

"Another approach we could take is to apply for a contributory parent visa, Subclass 173. This would be quicker, but would require what's called an assurance of support."

Ethel cocked an eyebrow, "Sounds expensive."

"It is, your sponsor will be expected to make a significant financial contribution to your future health and welfare costs."

"How significant?"

"$10,000 Australian dollars in the form of a bond paid to the Australian Government which will be kept for 10 years."

"They're afraid they're going to be lumbered with me."

"Your children?"

She withdrew her hands from the table and drew herself up, "No, the Australian Government."

"Well, in a nutshell, yes. The assurance of support scheme ensures your welfare costs are met by your sponsor rather than the Australian public. Your sponsor will make a commitment to provide financial support to you so that you won't have to rely on social welfare payments. They also commit to repay any welfare payments made to you during the assurance of support period."

"The 10 years?"

"Yes, and this is in addition to the $10,000 AUD bond."

"So one of my kids would have to take this on?"

"Your sponsor is normally one of your children but it doesn't have to be, the main requirement is that your sponsor is an Australian citizen."

"Is that all?"

"No, the financial commitment doesn't stop there. The lodgment fees for this visa are very high, $44,480 Australian dollars in total."

Ethel thought for a moment, "No," she said, "I'm not wild about that one either. What else is there?"

"Unfortunately that's it for permanent residency. Your other option is a tourist visa."

"I've been out to Australia on one of those before. They only last 3 months."

"That is the case for normal tourists visas but this is where the strategy I mentioned earlier comes in. If you have applied for a parent visa, subclass 103, and are in the queue for processing . . ."

"This is the queue that takes 10 years?"

". . . yes that queue, you can be granted a special tourist visa called a sponsored family visitor visa, subclass 679. This visa is valid for 5 years and you can stay for up to 12 months at a time on each entry. You will be expected to spend some time away from Australia between each entry but you won't have to apply for a new visa when you return."

"How does that help, I'll always be a visitor?"

"The main way it helps you is that it allows you to spend prolonged periods of time with your family in Australia. There are no bridging visas granted to applicants waiting for the outcome of a Parent visa, Subclass 103 application, which means that the only visa you could go and see your family on would be a standard tourist visa. The family visitor visa, on the other hand, allows you to see your family for up to 12 months at a time while you're waiting for your Parent visa, Subclass 103 application, to process."

Ethel was silent for a full minute evaluating my advice. Eventually she said, "So it sounds like the practical option for me is to apply for the parent visa and get myself in the queue, then while I'm waiting, use the family visitor visa to go and see my kids."

"Yes," I said. "I think that is your best option. Once the Parent visa is finally granted you will still need to meet the other criteria, Police clearances and health checks and so on, and you will still need a sponsor but the lodgment fees are much less, at the moment they are $3,855 Australian dollars but who knows what they'll be in 10 years."

"Who knows where any of us will be in 10 years," Ethel said smiling at me.

## 17 Student Visas

Pranav called me in a flurry, "I really must speak to you Mrs. Dalton. My student visa will expire in 36 days and I have found no employment yet."

Pranav was 28 years old, an Indian national, and had been studying IT in Sydney for the last 4 years. I had first spoken to him before he embarked on his study. He already had a degree in business but there was no demand for this in Australia at the time. In exploring his visa options the subject of retraining came up. He was very keen on this idea, as he loved studying.

Under the current requirements an Australian qualification counts for 5 more points in a points test. With an average pass mark of 60 points, 5 points is almost 10% of the required mark. As Pranav had the means to go to Australia to study I suggested that he do that and we could check his eligibility again once his studies were complete.

Pranav went off to complete an IT degree in Sydney and I didn't hear any more from him for 4 years.

## Which Student Visa?

There are a number student visas in the Australian visa system. What you intend to study will influence which student visa you apply for.

For the younger age group there is the primary or secondary school course visa - subclass 571. This is used mostly for children attending boarding school and the one I was on myself when I attended boarding school in New South Wales.

For people like Pranav the vocational education and training visa - subclass 572, and the higher education visa - subclass 573, are very popular. These cover Bachelor's Degrees, Associate Degrees, Graduate Certificates, Graduate Diplomas, Higher Education Diplomas, Higher Education Advanced Diplomas or Masters by coursework. For students pursuing a Masters Degree by research or a Doctoral Degree there is the postgraduate research visa - subclass 574.

You don't have to do a course that results in an Australian award, non-award foundation studies, or other full-time courses or components of courses are covered by the non-award visa - subclass 575.

If the Australian Government Overseas Aid Program (AUSAID), or the Australian Department of Defense is sponsoring you, these bodies are covered under the AUSAID and Defense visa - subclass 576.

## Can You Work?

All the visas above allow for 40 hours of work per fortnight once your course has commenced. The priority is your studies but the part-time work can help international students with work experience, or money, or both.

## Application

The method of applying for a student visa is primarily determined by what country you are from. The Australian Government has determined an assessment level for each country, ranging from Level 1 for those countries whose citizens pose the lowest immigration risk and Level 5 where citizens of certain countries are considered to represent a high immigration risk. The risk being that the applicant will overstay and become an illegal immigrant. Applicants from the UK and Ireland are on Assessment Level 1 and therefore have the option of applying online, by post, or in person for the main student visas.

## Requirements

For the visas mentioned above the requirements are as follows: -

- You must be accepted for full-time study in a registered course or part of a registered course.
- You must be a "Genuine Temporary Entrant" and demonstrate your intention to return home following completion of your study.
- You must have the capacity to cover the cost of airfares, course tuition fees and living costs for the duration of your stay in Australia, and demonstrate that these funds will be available to you in Australia.
- You must present evidence of your academic record.
- You must meet the character and health requirements.
- You must have adequate health insurance.

## Family

Your parents can apply for a visa to stay in Australia as your guardians under the Student Guardians Visa - Subclass 580. They will need to demonstrate they have the capacity to cover the cost of airfares, living costs and school tuition costs for all family unit members including you for the duration of their stay in Australia

Alternatively members of your family may apply for a student subclass 570–576 visa to live with you in Australia as your family.

Prior to the 1st of July 2012, you had to go offshore if you were on a student visa and wanted to apply for a general skilled migration visa. This is why Parnav was now calling me in a flap.

I explained to him about the new Skilled - Graduate (temporary) visa subclass 485, which allows overseas students who don't meet the criteria for a permanent General Skilled Migration visa to remain in Australia for 18 months to gain skilled work experience or improve their English language skills.

Parnav was very happy and relieved to hear this advice. As a holder of this visa, he could apply for permanent residence at any time if he is able to meet the pass mark on the General Skilled Migration points test.

### Strategy

If you are on a student visa you can apply for the 18 month graduate visa subclass 485 which will enable you to stay in Australia and work on either your work experience or getting a proficient IELTS test result which will facilitate a full skilled visa application in the next 18 month period.

## 18 Business Visas

"So all I need is a million dollars?" Pete asked reaching for his wallet. I thought for a moment he was going to start pulling out bank notes.

"Relax Megan," he said chuckling, "I'm just getting the number of my accountant."

"It's Mege," I replied, "remember, sounds like Peggy but with an "M.""

"Oh, yeah, right, Medge, got it," Pete said distractedly rummaging through his wallet.

I liked Pete, in spite of his mispronunciation of my name, which I'm sure he did on purpose to get a rise out of me. Pete had achieved a lot in his life. Starting from nothing he had built a multi million pound business through hard work and savvy business dealings. Now in his early fifties he was planning to move his family to Australia.

Though the business visa process is the most complex of all the visa categories Pete was, like most business people I act for, undaunted. For them it is just another series of tasks they need to work through.

"How much money you need," I continued, "will depend on what visa you apply for. For example, if you wanted to apply for the significant investor stream of the Provisional Business Innovation and Investment Visa, subclass 188, you would need 5 million."

"Australian?"

"Yes, it's always Australian dollars Pete," Pete turned slightly grey as he did the conversion to sterling in his head, "But I don't think that is the visa subclass for you. I think of that subclass as being for the super rich."

"Right."

"For business people like yourself, the process is in two stages. The first stage is a Provisional Business Innovation and Investment Visa, subclass 188 . . . "

"But you just said I needed to be super rich and have 5 million Aussie dollars lying about for that."

I smiled at Pete and sat back in my chair, "Here's the thing Pete. Prior to the middle of 2012 there were roughly 15 visa subclasses that related to business migration. That has now been simplified to 3 main subclasses with roughly 3 streams in each subclass. I'm happy to spend our time going through the merits of the Venture Capital Entrepreneur stream and how it compares to the Significant Business History stream or how the Provisional Investor stream transitions into the Permanent Investor stream subclass 888. I can do that, or I can spend our time going through which visa is going to suit you and what the steps are."

"Fair enough," Pete said holding his hands up in mock surrender and laughing

"As I was saying, it's going to be a two part process for you. The first part is a Provisional Business Innovation and Investment Visa subclass 188 – Business Innovation Stream."

"Different stream, got it."

"I'll just run through the broad strokes of what the requirements are, biggest one first. Do you or your wife have assets in excess of $800,000 AUD that you can transfer to Australia within two years of your visa being granted?"

Pete rubbed his chin mentally adding up his assets.

"Let me put that another way, " I said, "Do you plan on selling your house when you move to Australia?"

"Yes." said Pete, his face brightening.

"Is you house worth more than $800,000 AUD?"

"Easily."

"Okay so you meet that criteria. Has your business had an annual turnover of more than $500,000 AUD for 2 out of the last 4 years?"

"Yes."

"And you own more than 51% of the business?"

"Yes."

"Well those are the main criteria. As far as the conditions of the visa go you have to commit to maintaining an ownership interest in the new Australian company and have a direct and ongoing involvement in its management. You also have to meet the health and character requirements but other than that the only other condition of this stream is that you have to be nominated by a State."

"What does that mean in practice?"

"Well you want to live in Sydney, right?"

"Yes."

"That means you have to be nominated by the New South Wales Government."

"Assuming I do get a nomination from the New South Wales Government does that mean I have to stay in New South Wales?"

"Yes it means you have to stay there for at least 4 years."

"Okay, I'll have a think about that one but I don't think it should be a problem. You said there were two stages to the process, what's involved in the second stage?"

"Once you've been on the Provisional Business

Innovation and Investment Visa, subclass 188 – Business Innovation Stream, for two years you can apply for a Permanent Business Innovation and Investment Visa, subclass 888 – Business Innovation Stream."

"Right, what are the requirements for that, my first male child?"

"Nothing so drastic, you have demonstrate that you've had direct involvement in the management of the new Australian business. You need to show that the business had a turnover, of at least $300,000 AUD in the year before you apply. You need to own at least 30% of the business and you need to have complied with all the tax requirements for the business with the Australian Taxation Office."

"Sounds straightforward enough."

"You will also be required to show the net value of your assets and a history of your employment."

"Assets in Australia?"

"Yes, business and personal. The net value of your assets in the Australian business must be at least $200,000 AUD and the net value of your personal and business assets in Australia together must be at least $600,000 AUD for the year before you apply."

"And that would include whatever house we bought in Australia?"

"It would."

"That should be easy enough. You mentioned something about employment history?"

"Yes, for the year before you apply, you need to show that the Australian business has employed at least two full-time employees who are Australian citizens, permanent residents, or New Zealand passport holders."

"And that's it?"

I nodded.

Pete whistled, "That's all there is to it."

"Yes Pete, that's all there is to it."

Pete moved his family to Sydney the following year buying a mobile windscreen repair franchise. A year later we successfully lodged his application for his Permanent Business Innovation and Investment Visa, Subclass 888 in the Business Innovation Stream. He and his family are now permanent residents and Pete assures me that if I'm ever in Sydney and I get a crack in my windscreen he will, "look after me."

The process I have just outlined with Pete is just one example of a pathway in the business visa subclasses, granted it is the most common pathway but it is definitely not the only one.

### Getting the Right Help

Business visas are the most complex of all the visa categories and if you think a business visa is right for you I strongly urge you to use the services of a registered migration agent. Having said that not all registered migration agents will undertake business visas. In fact many agents will pale noticeably if you start asking them about business visas. If you persist they will change the subject and try and get away from you as fast as possible, so I urge you to find an agent who has experience in business visas.

Speaking from personal experience, business visas draw on all the agents experience, skill and creativity to find the best pathway for the client and help them navigate any hurdle they may encounter on the way.

An agent with experience in business visas is crucial because business visas require careful strategy if they are going to be successful. For example, this is particularly relevant to the pathway I outlined for Pete, because if the provisional visa, the subclass 188, is not prepared correctly it can short circuit any chance of transitioning to the permanent subclass 888 successfully.

One last point is that many small business owners assume that the business visa is the obvious option for them. This is often not the case. This is because the turnover thresholds for the current business visas often exclude the smaller business owner. For example the minimum turnover threshold is $500,000 AUD and the minimum asset threshold is $400,000 AUD.

If you are a small business owner but your turnover or asset level don't reach these thresholds you will need to find another way to achieve your dream of living and working in Australia.

More than with any other visa category, for business visas, using the services of a registered migration agent is vital, but as I said there are horses for courses and it is equally important that you use a migration agent who has experience in the business visa process.

# Section 4    Further Considerations

## *19 Illegal Immigrant*

I was between meetings and sitting in a coffee shop near Bondi beach when my phone rang. The voice on the other end of the phone was Irish, female, and shaky.

"Mrs. Dalton?"

"Yes. How can I help you."

"I was given your number by a friend. I want to get a visa."

"I see, well if you give my office a call we can take all your details then do a full visa assessment for you to see what your options are, then you can come in for a chat about how to . . ."

"I'm not far away but I'd rather not meet you in person."

"I see. How long have you overstayed your visa?"

There was a long silence on the other end of the phone, "Is it that obvious?"

"Well let's just say you're not the first person to call me about overstaying. How long have you overstayed?"

"10 months," the woman said, her voice cracking, "it's too much man, I can't stand the stress any more, I'm always looking over my shoulder waiting for the immigration Police. It's really bringing me down. I want to get legal."

"I understand it must be awful. Well the first thing I have to tell you is that you'll have to leave the country."

"What?"

"I'm sorry but the Department of Immigration are very cut and dried about this. If you overstay your visa you have to leave the country."

"But isn't there, like, some kind of visa I can get to allow me to stay?"

"You can be issued a short bridging visa to give you time to leave the country, but that's all."

"When you say short are we talking months?"

"No, weeks at the most."

"Oh man, am I going to be arrested?"

"No, but you will need to present yourself to the Immigration Department. They have a special unit that deals with people who have overstayed; it's called the Community Status Resolution Service, or CSRS for short. You can contact them anonymously on 1300 853 773, but really you will need visit them in person."

"Where would I have to go?"

"The CSRS are located at Department of Immigration offices in all major Australian cities. When you present yourself they can issue you with a bridging visa E, which will make you lawful while you are leaving the country."

"Oh man, will I be banned for life then? I really love living here."

"No you won't be banned for life, just 3 years."

"And I can't get a visa for during that time?"

"Not any of the temporary visas like a tourist visa, or a 457 visa, or a working holiday visa, or . . . "

"That's what I came over on, a working holiday visa."

"Did you extend it to the second year?"

"Yeah, I did some fruit picking near Nimbin in my first year and I really liked the vibe in the whole Byron bay area, so I just went from job to job in Byron after that till I started working here, it's a kind of a craft gallery coffee shop. It's got great energy."

"I'm sure it has."

"I ended up kind of running the place. The guy who owns it is a bit of a hippie and he really dug my marketing ideas. The place started making money so he was happy. He never really checked the expiry date on my visa and by the time it ran out, like, I was the person in charge of checking that sort of thing so I just let it slide and kind of stayed on."

"I see. Do you have any formal qualifications?"

"Yeah, they're a total drag. You've probably never heard of it but I'm a qualified Marketing Specialist. That's what I was doing before I came to Australia."

"Actually, I have heard of Marketing Specialist, it's one of the occupations on the Consolidated Sponsored Occupations List or CSOL for short."

"For Australia?"

"Yes, for Australia."

"That's fantastic! No, wait, what does that mean?"

"It means you may be able to apply for a skilled visa as a Marketing Specialist."

"That's amazeballs! So that means I wouldn't have to leave the country."

"No, you will still have to leave the country."

"Aw no, this conversation is a trip. It's like a high, then a low, then a high, then like . . ."

"A low?"

"Hello?"

"Hello."

"I think you broke up there for a bit."

"Em, okay."

"So you're saying I still have to leave the country - bummer, but I can apply for a visa - which is awesome, but I can't apply for 3 years – bummer again. Is that right?"

"Not completely. You can't apply for a temporary visa but you can apply for a skilled permanent visa. The 3 year ban doesn't apply to permanent visas."

"Wow, check it, are you saying I could leave Australia and apply for a visa as soon as I get back to Ire . . , I mean the country that-I-came-to-Australia-from?"

"Yes, when you get back to Ireland you could start. . ."

"Wow, that's wild man, are you like psychic or what? How did you?"

"Know you're from Ireland?"

"Like, yeah?"

"We've known about you for some time. In fact we're watching you right now."

"What?"

"Just kidding, I could tell from your accent. You know we are based in Ireland, right?"

"Aw don't man, you totally freaked me out."

"Sorry, couldn't resist. Getting back to what I was saying, when you get back to Ireland come in and see us and we will assess you to see if you meet the criteria. If you do we can start the application process."

"Will the fact that I'm illegal go against me?"

"Well it won't help but we can explain the reason you overstayed when we make your application. It will be up to the case officer dealing with your application to decide."

"How long will all that take?"

"At the moment, skilled visas are processing in about 3 - 6 months."

"No way."

"Pardon?"

"Are you saying I could be back in Australia in 6 months?"

"Theoretically it is possible but we would need to assess you properly first to see if you will meet the criteria, then the case officer dealing with your application will need to be understanding about your overstaying. So there is a lot that needs to happen . . ."

"I-am-soo-glad-I-CALLED-YOU!!!"

"O-kay."

"What was that number again I'm going to call that CS

. . . whatever, crowd right now."

"Call in person remember. That will be a trip to Brisbane for you."

"Right. No worries. So I'll give you a shout when I'm back in Dublin. My Mum will be delighted to see me. I haven't been able to go home since I've been illegal."

"That will be nice. Okay I'll talk to you back in Dublin."

"Thanks a million."

### Further Considerations

The conversation I had with my mystery caller is standard for a certain kind of overstaying. The economic prospects in the country of origin, Ireland in this case, are bleak so they don't want to return, but they can't stay in Australia either. While they are trying to figure out what to do the expiry date on their visa slips past and they overstay.

### Refugee and Asylum

There is a whole other group of people who overstay their visa because they can't return to their country of origin. I have in the past worked with a Brisbane based organization called Refugee and Immigration Legal Services, or RAILS for short. RAILS offer free legal advice in immigration and refugee cases to people in need. You can find out more details on their website www.rails.org.au

There is also the International Organisation for Migration, or IOM for short. IOM is an independent, global organization, which provides impartial information to people in this situation. You can contact IOM directly from anywhere in Australia on 1300 116 986.

### Strategy

The strategy for overstaying your visa is really simple – don't. There is a 28 day grace period for most temporary visas so if you leave before that time, in most cases, there won't be a re-entry ban issued against you.

If you have overstayed beyond the 28 day period, the strategy is simple again - leave the country. You are not obliged to present yourself to the Department of Immigration before you leave but if you want to avoid potential unpleasant scenes at the airport I strongly advise that you do.

Present yourself to the CSRS so you can leave the country lawfully. You will still get a re-entry ban but should you apply for a visa in the future it will stand you in good stead that you left the country lawfully.

## 20 Migration Agents

"They charged you how much?"

"$6,000."

"And you haven't heard from them in how long?"

"9 months."

"And they were applying for a spouse visa on your behalf?"

"That's right."

"I'm sorry Patricia, but it doesn't sound good."

Patricia swallowed and blinked, "You mean my visa won't get approved."

"No, I mean it sounds like you've been ripped off."

### Choosing a Migration Agent

As ridiculous as that conversation may sound, I've had far too many like it in my time as a migration agent. The sad fact about getting assistance with Australian visa applications is there are a lot of fraudulent operators out there.

The first step in finding a legitimate migration agent is easy enough. All Australian migration agents must be registered with the Migration Agent Registration

Authority, or MARA for short. This is a great safeguard for you because it makes it very simple for you to check the authenticity of your prospective migration agent. All registered migration agents are listed on the MARA website - www.mara.gov.au

When you are searching on the internet and you come across a migration agent, or a migration expert, or a visa specialist, or a visa agent, or a migration specialist, or any of the many other creative names you will come across, and you will come across them, you can very easily check it to see if your prospective agent is on the list. If they're not on the list, they're not obliged to adhere to a professional code of conduct, so best to be avoided. It's as simple as that.

The Australian Government is so serious about this that it is actually a criminal offence in Australia to offer migration advice professionally if you are not registered with MARA.

The next step is not so easy because once you have established that your prospective migration agent is registered with MARA you need to figure out if they are a good fit for you.

What is a good fit for you will be determined by a number of considerations, everything from customer service, to price, to personalities. In my experience the overriding attribute people look for in a migration agent is success. The question being, "What are the chances of this agent getting my visa approved?"

Answering that question for yourself is not easy. The ideal situation will be if you get a referral from someone, you know and trust, who has used the services of the prospective agent and were happy with the result.

If you don't know someone who has used the prospective agent then the next best thing are testimonials from previous clients. Testimonials may sound trivial and a bit corny, but I have found they are a good barometer of the agent's track record.

In my own case my clients are more than happy to write testimonials once they get their visa approval. Many write them spontaneously. I think this is because moving country is such an emotional roller coaster that when the visa is finally granted there is a huge outpouring of positive emotion and gratitude.

If you are a migration agent and you don't have any testimonials or you can't at least have some previous clients that prospective clients can talk to then I think that speaks volumes about your track record.

### Fees

On the MARA website there is a good guide for what the range of migration agent fees should be. It gives you an idea of the price range you should be paying for the type of visa you are interested in.

It is worth pointing out again that migration agent fees will always be small in comparison to the lodgment fees you will have to pay to the Australian Government, and if you remember, the lodgment fees you pay to the Australian Government are non-refundable. Choosing a migration agent based on price alone is a false economy and is frequently regretted.

### Free Visa Assessments

Visa application fees are expensive and as I mentioned earlier, non refundable. I am all for being prudent when it comes to spending money and it's important to spot a good deal when you see one, but in my experience, "Free Visa Assessments!" are never a good deal.

It is a proven marketing strategy to broadcast the word, "Free," in your marketing message. It is attention grabbing and encourages people to engage without any risk. Normally we can see this kind of sales shtick coming a mile away. If you are driving down the street and see a sign for a, "Free Oil Change!," outside an auto mechanics, I think most people would know that the oil change will probably end up costing them something one way or another. When it comes to a complicated process like visa applications the sales shtick can be harder to see.

Needless to say I don't do free visa assessments.

### Trust

While it is always nice to be able to drop in and see your agent in person, with modern communications it is not necessary. I have clients from all around the world. Most of the documentation is handled online and any of the face to face chats that need to happen are done via Skype video. The location of your prospective migration agent can often seem like a logical consideration but compared to trusting your migration agent, which I feel is crucial, location is a minor consideration, and here's why.

Once you have gathered all the information about a prospective migration agent and you have met them either personally or via Skype, and you are about to engage them as your agent, ask yourself this simple question, "Do I trust this person?"

If you answer, "No," then I recommend you move on until you find an agent you do trust.

The reason I stress this need for trust is that most visa

applications take a long time, months, and in some cases, years. If, for example, you haven't heard anything from the Department of Immigration in 8 weeks and your agent tells you this is normal, having trust in your agent will ease your mind and make the waiting easier.

If you don't have that trust in your agent it will make a difficult situation almost unbearable. I have seen the effects of this first hand when I have been asked to take over applications for clients who have come to the end of their tether with their previous migration agent. The high level of prolonged stress has drastic effects on these clients and affects every aspect of their lives, from health, to relationships, to finances.

Trusting your migration agent is crucial.

# 21 Citizenship

"I want to become an Australian citizen. How do I do it?"

"Well, the first thing you have to do Wolfgang, is become an Australian permanent resident."

"No, I'm not interested in a permanent resident, I want to become a citizen."

"I see. Just to be clear, you are intending to live in Australia, right?"

"Ah yes. I want to live in Australia."

"Permanently?"

"Yes, for good."

"Okay, then the first thing you have to do is become a permanent resident."

"Why with the permanent resident all the time when I want to be a citizen?"

"It's the first stage in the process Wolfgang. It's not possible to become an Australian citizen without first becoming a permanent resident."

"I see. How long do I have to be a permanent resident?"

"Normally 4 years."

"No. Too long."

"You don't really have a choice Wolfgang, that is the process. One of the requirements for Australian citizenship is that you have been living lawfully in Australia for 4 years on a valid Australian visa. You also must not have been absent from Australia for more than 1 year in total, in the 4 year period, including no more than 90 days in the year before making the application."

"I see, is there no other way?"

"Well unless you were born in Australia, or one of your parents is an Australian citizen?"

Wolfgang didn't respond but his face went red.

"Then no, there is no other way."

Wolfgang just sat there his face getting redder.

"What is it about being a permanent resident you don't like Wolfgang?"

"I want to work. I don't want to be no illegal."

"You can work as a permanent resident."

Wolfgang's eyebrows shot up, "I can?"

"Yah, I mean yes, yes you can work. As a permanent resident you can remain in Australia indefinitely, you have full work rights, and you are even eligible for the Australian health insurance, which is called Medicare."

"Good. But wait, if it is so good to be a permanent resident why does anyone become a citizen?"

"Well there are some things only a citizen can do, like voting, for example, or running for public office, or serving on a jury, or holding an Australian passport. Also as an Australian permanent resident you have to renew your permanent residency every 5 years, but as an Australian citizen you wouldn't have to do that."

Wolfgang sat back and looked at the floor. He began to say something a number of times then stopped.

"In my experience," I said, "the decision to become an

Australian citizen has more to do with the heart than the head. It is a way of making your choice to belong to the Australian community official, at least that's what it was for me and I know my husband, John, felt the same way about it when . . . "

"Okay, I become a permanent resident, and then I become a citizen 4 years later. It sounds like a lot of good things for just filling in a form to get a passport."

"Well there's a little more to it than that Wolfgang. To become an Australian citizen you must first pass a citizenship test."

"A test?"

"Yes, the citizenship test is a computer based multiple choice test consisting of 20 questions drawn at random from a pool of questions. To pass the test, you must answer 15 out of 20 questions, correctly."

"Questions, what kind of questions?"

"The questions are about Australia's democratic beliefs, the rights and liberties of its people, Australian Government, and the law in Australia. All the questions are covered on the Department of Immigration and Citizenship website - www.citizenship.gov.au"

"Okay so then I get the passport."

"No, once you have passed the citizenship test you must then attend a citizenship ceremony where you make your pledge of commitment to Australia."

"My pledge . . . at a ceremony? What pledge?"

I stood up and placed my hand on my heart. Looking into the distance I said, "From this time forward, under God, I pledge my loyalty to Australia and its people, whose democratic beliefs I share, whose rights and liberties I respect, and whose laws I will uphold and obey," looking down at Wolfgang I said, "You can choose whether or not to use the words 'under God'." If you guessed I was getting a bit tired of Wolfgang's grubby attitude to becoming an Australian citizen, you were right. Wolfgang just looked at me with his mouth open.

Sitting down again I continued, "Citizenship ceremonies can be small, my own ceremony had just one other new citizen, or they can be very large, at my husband John's ceremony there were over a thousand people. The larger ceremonies can be very celebratory affairs with representatives of the Indigenous people and other local community leaders and representatives. There can be music and speeches but all ceremonies involve the pledge because you don't become an Australian citizen until you make your pledge of commitment."

"Okay, I go for it."

"That's great Wolfgang. There is one last thing about becoming an Australian citizen that you should know. Australia allows dual citizenship meaning you can hold two passports. My husband, John, for example, holds two passports as he is an Irish citizen, and he is also an Australian citizen."

"That is good."

"The thing is Wolfgang, you can only hold dual citizenship if both countries allow dual citizenship."

Wolfgang just kept looking at me.

"Germany doesn't Wolfgang, Germany doesn't allow dual citizenship."

Wolfgang was silent for a moment, "What does that mean?" he asked eventually.

"It means that you will have to forfeit your German passport if you become an Australian citizen."

"Never!" he said standing up, "I will never give up my German citizenship."

"That is your choice Wolfgang, perhaps being a permanent resident would be the best option for you then."

"Yes, permanent resident but not citizen."

As you can gather I am very proud to be Australian and would encourage you to pursue Australian citizenship only if you intend to embrace the Australian community and all it stands for.

# Conclusion

I hope you have enjoyed this book and are a little clearer on what is involved in the process of attaining a visa to Australia. I also hope I have demystified some of the more convoluted regulations and criteria and have helped you begin to develop a practical strategy for your plans to make Australia your new home.

It goes without saying that I strongly encourage you to get in touch with a registered migration agent to get some professional advice about your visa options. I know my team and I would love to hear from you, if you would like to get in touch with us you can do so through my website. www.TheImmigrationAgency.com

Australia is such a fantastic country to live in it requires no selling on my part as it sells itself. The people, the lifestyle, and the opportunities make it such an attractive option.

I wish you all the best in your dream of living and working in Australia and look forward to welcoming you to the country.

Mege Dalton

# About the author

Mege Dalton is a native of Papua New Guinea. Educated in Australia she became an Australian citizen in 2006. She graduated from the University of Papua New Guinea in 2001 with a Bachelor of Law and began work as a commercial litigation lawyer.

In 2005 she moved to Brisbane where she graduated from the Queensland University of Technology and was admitted to the Bar in Queensland. She went on to become a registered migration agent specialising in migration law.

In 2006 she moved to Ireland with her Irish husband John. Wanting to put her own mark on the migration industry she founded The Immigration Agency in Dublin in 2008 and since then has been helping people migrate to Australia from Ireland, the United Kingdom, India, the United Arab Emirates, South Africa and many other countries.

It is her vision to provide excellent visa services to anyone who would like to emigrate to Australia. She is also passionate about helping clients to decide if applying for an Australian visa is right for them by providing an abundance of information and resources about the Australian immigration system.

In her spare time she is an avid squash player and can be found at least once a week down at the RTE sports club playing a few games with friends. She loves to cook, plays the guitar and yes, she has two cats.

Index

# A.

# B.

# C